Somewhere In Montana

A Spiritual Awakening In Blackfeet Country

Bill Joseph, I understand you ARE
A MAN who has touched the hearts of
MAN because of your ExAmple... Always
show your love To those who NEED A
helping heand and. you will change Their
world!
Blessings

Bill Old Chief

Bill
Old Chief   4/16/16

WESTBOW
PRESS®
A DIVISION OF THOMAS NELSON
& ZONDERVAN

WestBow Press books may be ordered through booksellers or by contacting:

WestBow Press
A Division of Thomas Nelson & Zondervan
1663 Liberty Drive
Bloomington, IN 47403
www.westbowpress.com
1 (866) 928-1240

ISBN: 978-1-5127-2889-7 (sc)
ISBN: 978-1-5127-2890-3 (hc)
ISBN: 978-1-5127-2888-0 (e)

Library of Congress Control Number: 2015919467

Print information available on the last page.

WestBow Press rev. date: 3/02/2016

Contents

*"That which was intended for evil,
God turned into a blessing"*

Dedication

As I begin this book the first person that I must acknowledge is my wife Muriel whom I have loved since high school. She has blessed me with four awesome children and many grandchildren, which we continue to count. At times we have journeyed through ominous spiritual valleys as husband and wife and stood upon the mountaintops of our victories as one...truly what God has joined together, let no man put asunder.

She is a woman of God who has helped direct my many endeavors and especially the writing of this book. She has been able to often see with clarity and counsel through the Word of God the challenges I have encountered throughout our life...she has a way of conveying calm and reassurance to most situations that others would shutter at.

Muriel's encouragement to write what God has given me and what I have learned as a Christian who was raised on the Blackfeet Indian Reservation in northern Montana now transfers to your life. Since life is a gift given from God, I now give you this gift from my heart and pray that you grow in the grace of God just as I have.

Secondly I dedicate these words to future generations who will cultivate their lives on the Blackfeet Indian Reservation. Browning is a tough place to live but I call it home for there is no other place like it that I have visited. Each morning you are greeted by the glory and splendor of God through his creation called the Great Plains, prairies that extend eastward as far as the eye can see and the Rocky Mountain Front, better known as the "Backbone of the Continent."

The people exemplify the spirit of our past warriors who dared to venture beyond our traditional boundaries in search of adventure and opportunity. The harshness of the land and the elements of severe weather changes produce individuals of character, strength, and inspiration. The best quality of the Blackfeet people is that they have learned to laugh during times of adversity they find humor in everything.

The third person is Pastor Dean Buffalo of "Spirit of God Church" Assembly of God, Ronan, Montana. In the few short years that I have known him and his wife Annie I have been encouraged beyond mere words. Pastor Dean is a man of commitment, dedication, and love for the displaced. I have seen him mature from a young minister into a seasoned leader who motivates the lives of young and old through his ability to connect to their hearts. Those with integrity stand tall among the crowd; Pastor Dean is such a man.

In a time of my life that I was displaced and even rejected by some, Pastor Dean Buffalo opened his pulpit to our ministry month after month, and now years. Because of his unconditional love I have grown into a better person who has committed my life to reaching others for Jesus. Blessed are they whose iniquities are forgiven and whose sins are covered (Romans 4:7). The people of the Flathead Indian Reservation are better off because of Pastor Dean and Annie. He truly is a man of compassion and vision.

Preface By: Muriel Old Chief

It is with great pleasure that I write this introduction for my husband Bill, whom I have the utmost love and respect. I thank God everyday for blessing me with a husband, who loves the Lord, he is truly a man after Gods own heart.

Bill's parents would always invite us to go to the Full Gospel revivals and camp meetings that were held around the reservation his father Grayson was well known preacher throughout. Indian country. Once in a while we would go but leave as soon as the music portion was over and I would say to him "Why are we leaving"? Bill would always say, "I am not ready." There was a Full Gospel church about 2 blocks from our tiny apartment, and on a Wednesday night we walked through the doors and we were never the same again as Bill and I got "saved" that night on May 21, 1980.

Every evening when Bill would come home from work he went right to the closet in our bedroom and began to pray. Before this time some people would say he was quiet and it was difficult for him to talk to people unless of course he knew them. As he prayed I could hear him asking God to give him the boldness to speak and for God to use him and I could here him say "I surrender everything to you Lord".

I never saw anybody so hungry for knowledge Bill would read all the time he read and studied his Bible every chance he got, he studied all subjects of the Bible sought the Lord for everything we had need of as our family grew. His most quoted scripture at that time was **II Timothy 2:15 Study to show thyself approved unto God, a workman that needeth not to be ashamed, rightly dividing the word of truth.**

He not only studied Gods Word but he also read all types of books he was so hungry for knowledge one time he bought some old encyclopedias at a yard sale and read them like he was reading a novel. Whenever any of our children would ask me about a subject I would say, "Ask your dad he knows everything"! And I really meant it.

As Bill began to preach, teach, hold bible studies, Pastor, and evangelize where God led him he started writing things down and I would read them and would be so blessed by the messages and to hear the stories of his growing up years. I knew the Lord wanted him to share his experiences. The stories and testimonies you are about to read will surely awaken something within you. During times of testing, uncertainty, death, and hardships you will be able to stay faithful and the joy of the Lord will be your strength.

By his steadfastness and diligent desire to be a workman approve of God he has taken our family on a journey I will forever praise the Lord for.

With great love and respect,
Muriel Old Chief

Introduction

Today I encouraged my mother Irene in the Word as I have during each visit to her home. As a child she taught me how to pray. As a Prodigal Son she showed me the way home. As an ordained minister, Pastor, Evangelist, and Teacher she instilled the Word of God into my life and encouraged me through her example as a woman who loves the Lord. I deem it vital to provide spiritual opportunity for her future according the promises written in the Bible even if we live in a darken world that seems to have encompassed our daily lives.

Everywhere a person looks today we are reminded of death, destruction, and despair. The days of certainty have been replaced with fear. I'm reminded of a song that said, "Momma, tell me about the good ol' days.' We no longer live in a world influenced by the painter, "Norman Rockwell" as small children stroll peacefully through the countryside with grandpa.

While confined as slaves to Egypt the children of Israel were instructed by Moses that a day of breakthrough was soon approaching and to get ready. He reminded them that God was about to release his blessing upon them and even though trouble was coming to the land He would keep them protected. "When I see the blood I will pass over you." When the blood of Jesus is applied to your heart, your mind, and your body God will see you through.

The Word of God is a book of breakthroughs, breakouts, and crossing over to the other side. It is a book that details the lives of ordinary individuals who have had supernatural encounters with the Creator while traveling their symbolic road of "normality and uninteresting beginnings."

As a young man David must have often felt alone and forgotten in the backside of the desert while he watched over his father's sheep. As David accepted the challenge of Goliath he was reminded of the lion and bear he killed in the wilderness... he recalled the Word of God is the same yesterday, today, and forever and if God had given him victory in the past surely God would prevail today against the giant that stood before him. Who would have realized that God was preparing him to one day be king of Israel?

As you examine your life while reading this book you too will recall the bear or the lion that God gave you victory over in the 'desert times' of your life. Get ready to cross over and breakout into what God has called you to be. Just as change came over Jacob because he refused to let go...your change is coming according to the Word of God.

What people called you in the past does not reflect what God calls you now. He told Jacob, "You will no longer be called Jacob (supplanter ~ trickster ~ deceiver ~ failure) but you will now be called Israel (a prince among men)...greatness is about to come out of you. Look for it. Expect it. Get ready for it. Don't despise the day of small beginnings, for without a vision you will perish but in a multitude of counselors there is safety.

Pastor Bill Old Chief

CHAPTER ONE

What do they call you?

In the Old Testament there is a story of a man that was displaced, confused, and rejected however, there was a promise from God concerning his life. Like the Prodigal Son of the New Testament he thought his life was unimportant to others and that his actions would merely affect himself. I once read that our action will impact at least twenty other individuals in one way or another. Consider the alcoholic or drug abuser that lose their jobs, destroy their marriages, and reject their children. The ripple effect is felt for years and changes the lives of parents, grandparents…their entire environment is altered because they have chosen to destroy all that is important to them.

In Genesis 25:26 we are introduced to Jacob, brother of Esau and the son of Isaac. In verse twenty-two even before his birth there is a strange occurrence taking place within his mother Rebecca that causes great concern. The Bible describes it as, "a struggle between the children" and after inquiring an answer from God she is told that there are "Two Nations" within her and "Two Manner of People."

Because of sin our lives begin with a struggle. It doesn't matter how cute you are at birth or how rich your family is. You may live in the best part of the country in the most beautiful home however, sin has a way of disfiguring or deforming our lives and one day that "cute little baby" is now a destructive, inconsiderate, self-centered individual that is only focused on serving their own personal needs and desires.

Jacob learns quickly that if he is to become anything in life he must make it happen for himself. According to Hebrew custom the eldest child (first born) was to obtain the birthright, which was Esau however, the struggle that begin within now begins to manifest outwardly for all to see. Rather than offer a meal to his brother Esau, Jacob uses the opportunity to steal his brother's birthright thus he is stealing his blessing. Esau is symbolic of a Christian that places no value on the Promises of God. He willing sold his promise from God for a bowl of soup and bread.

From this point on Jacob is despised by his brother and he realizes he must stay one step ahead of Esau if he is to truly capture his father's blessing. When a person conceives a lie, from the seed deception is produced and it often will involve others to complete the final result. We are told that Rebecca loved Jacob more than Esau. Her heart becomes deceived by pity for Jacob and she decides to assist Jacob in stealing the blessing from her eldest son Esau. It is interesting that Rebekah's name translates to "a rope, noose, as of a maiden who ensnares by her beauty."

Her deceit was the noose that would haunt Jacob for years to come. It would be the rope that tied him to his past, a past of shattered dreams, death, and isolation. The Bible tells us that promotion comes from God; you can't steal your promotion let alone a blessing from God. The entirety of this story can be found in the book of Genesis but it is the part that Jacob has a supernatural encounter that grabs my attention for it is here that change is about to happen and the depressing situation that Jacob has lived with for countless years is going to be replaced with just a few words from God as He asks the question, "What is thy name?" In other words what do they call you?

Before we answer the question let's look at Genesis 32: 24 which is one of the most profound scriptures I have ever read. **And Jacob was left alone**; every time I read this portion it stops me in my tracks as if you're listening for an echo in a distance valley. And Jacob was left alone indicates that he had come to the end of his symbolic rope. No more tricks to pull out of the bag. No more lies to cover his trail of tears. No more deception as he stands alone in a supernatural encounter with God.

Jacob is a picture of our past without Christ, it is only when we confess our true nature that we see our future as Jesus intended it to be. As long as a person chooses to cover their sin there will be struggle, contention, and guilt within their life. I will never move forward as long as I continue to look back. Sounds simple yet this is the most difficult decision that most people struggle with and it disables their ability to fulfill their destiny according to the Word of God.

You were created in the image of God, after His likeness...and God blessed you according to Genesis 1:26-28 however, as sin begin to grow in your life and you nurtured sin the things of God become less and less important. As a child I was dedicated to the Lord. At the age of accountability I was taught to honor God. I was taught to pray. And just like Jacob I begin to look for shortcuts in life that only produced disappointment.

We can relate this very situation to our coming to Christ as a repentant sinner because in most cases a person will testify later in their Christian life that they felt all alone and that their world came crashing in on them, and this is a true statement. When I first read this passage I was maturing in the Lord, I had been traveling extensively across the country preaching, singing, and experiencing the powerful hand of God in the lives of people. But I had come to the "end of my rope" concerning my spiritual walk and what I believed.

My focus had turned from the Word of God and what Jesus had done for me to the failures and shortcomings of others and this greatly affected my perception and ability to walk this walk of faith. My confession became that of a battle weary soldier...all I wanted to do was lay down like Elijah the prophet of old and let the angel feed me, pity me, or just hold me up. It is in these moments I am reminded of Moses who had to spend sometime in the backside of the desert. It was a place of isolation.

As human beings "isolation" is the thing we fear for the most part. As individuals age they become fearful concerning their healthcare, "Will I end up in a nursing home all alone?" As a child there fear is being forgotten along the roadside or in some major mall and separated from their family and for others isolation in the countryside is an intolerable lifestyle, they must live in the city even if it requires remaining strangers with those around them.

What is thy name? God already knew the answer to this question but he needed to hear it from Jacob. <u>Confession</u> is a key that enables God access in to our dire situations and the darken areas of our heart; Proverbs 28:13 (KJV) says, "He that coverers his sins shall not prosper: but whoso confesses and forsakes them shall have mercy."

What do they call you? That same question is being asked of you. It is being asked of those who have encountered your life. Some may know you as the person who's family were drunks. Others know you as a failure, swindler, deceitful, angry, overweight, oppressed, depressed, dysfunctional, bitter person, and on and on, and on. However they don't know what God calls you and the change that is about to take place in your life. All it takes is one word from God and your life will never be the same again. Your world is about to change. Joseph said, "That which was intended for evil, God turned into a blessing…that which was intended for evil, God turned into a blessing."

Genesis 32:2427 (NKJV) it is written:

> Then **Jacob was left alone**; and a Man wrestled with him
> until the breaking of day. Now when He saw that He did
> not prevail against him, He touched the socket of his hip;
> and the socket of Jacob's hip was out of joint as He wrestled
> with him. And He said, "Let Me go, for the day breaks."

But he said, "<u>**I will not let you go unless you bless me!**</u>"
So He said to him, "What *is* your name?"
He said, "Jacob."

The more I read this the more I am amazed how arrogant man is to think he can fight with God and win. There are times in our lives we will wrestle with God. It may be concerning a decision to go into the ministry or commit to your local church. Other times it involves personal issues that you refuse to share because of embarrassment or you may appear weak because you asked for help. And then there are the times God is just trying our will to see if we will obey Him. Whatever the case may be God will always win and it is ridiculous for us to think we can triumph over the God of all creation.

In our human pride we might think we have the answers to life. We may think our success lies in our education, our position, in our ability to reason. Jacob's nature was to deceive and the same could be said of us. How many times have we come before God only to speak half-truths, only to blame others…we wrestle with God yet, we want the full blessing of the Father without being transparent. James 4:6 says, "God resisteth the proud, but gives grace to the humble." Could it be that Jacob finally realized that all who he deemed important had forsaken him and his plans were just an illusion of his pride?

It doesn't matter who leaves us in life since friends and family come and go. But if God ever leaves us we are truly lost and alone. Three things were revealed because of the supernatural encounter with God. It's amazing how the Holy Spirit is able to take off the disguise of our lives as we surrender all unto Him. Isn't it even more amazing how God provides provision in the midst of our disparity, disappointment, and displacement?

What the songwriter wrote in the past, remains true today, "God looked beyond all my faults and saw my need." David said it even more eloquent in Psalms 94:18, "When my feet slipped, your mercy held me up." Mercy is God's kindness, favor, and goodness toward us...even if we didn't deserve it, His mercy will endure forever.

1. Jacob became desperate for God
2. Jacob presented himself broken before God
3. Jacob was honest with God

Proverbs 6:16 says there is six things that God hates and seven are an abomination (outrage) to him; a proud look or a spirit of pride tops the list. As Jacob's world comes crashing in on him there is no room for pride any more...he is alone, fearful, and crushed because of his prior actions. As he wrestles with God his true intentions are revealed and his past is exposed before God.

I imagine his mind going back to the days of his childhood as his father Isaac shared how God had been so good to them. How God had promised his grandparents a son in their old age, a miracle in it self since Abraham was 100 years old and Sarah was 90 years old. How could he not forget what the Lord had done for him and his family? As he wrestles he realizes he must hold on, "I can't let go, this might be my only and last chance for a breakthrough in my life"...so he holds on. I have said those very words a time or two, "Father God I will not let go until you bless me."

Envision for a moment, the sun is rising the wrestling is about to come to an end. The battle is just about over. No more tears in the mid-night hour. No more lies in the heat of the day. No more running from your true calling, your true destiny. People have called you everything in the book except BLESSED. It is said just before the breaking of the day, the night is the darkest and this is a dark time for Jacob.

God tells him, "Let me go" yet, Jacob refuses so God touches his thigh and causes Jacob to limp and to this Jacob replies, "I will not let you go until you bless me." It is here that we discover the answer to the question, "What is thy name?" What do they call you? They call me JACOB, which is, translated heel-catcher, supplanter, schemer, trickster, swindler…it is all the negative thoughts and words a person could use to be-little or degrade someone with. Even as a child Bishop T. D. Jake was known in his West Virginian neighborhood as "the bad Bible boy." He was also told he would never be able to preach. Words are powerful whether good or bad. The Bible tells us that life and death are in the power of the tongue.

Genesis 32:28, "And (God) he said, Thy name shall be no more Jacob, but Israel [having power with God or God's fighter]: for as a prince hast thou power with God and with men, and hast prevailed." God didn't take away the limp from Israel it became a cornerstone in his life concerning the mercy and forgiveness that only God is able to deliver. It was a reminder of the encounter he had with God. The trickster became a prince and greatness followed.

There are things that I have wrestled with during my Christian journey that has resulted in a spiritual limp, I don't dwell on it constantly however, it is a gentle reminder to me I had a encounter with God. In the times of my life that I may exhume pride or anything that isn't pleasing to God the spiritual limp becomes evident and I ask for his grace and mercy rather than sin. By His grace we are saved, restored, and set free! It is remarkable how many people I have encountered who have a spiritual limp and didn't know the reason why it happened. It reminds me of the young girl who became pregnant and said, "I don't know how it happen?" Now that may sound silly, but it's true.

"My sheep hear my voice, and I know them"

1 Chronicles 12:32, "And the children of Issachar, which were men had understanding of the times, to know what Israel ought to do." In other words they had discernment, wisdom, knowledge and the ability to know the plan of God concerning their life. In this walk it is vital to hear the voice of God in our spirit for without that ability we will not find our way. Jesus often spoke to the masses in a manner of transparency. He presented the Gospel in a fashion that brought men to conviction but he always provided an avenue for recourse concerning sin in their life. One example is when the woman was about to be stoned because she was caught in the act of adultery.

Just before the stones were to be tossed Jesus spoke these words, "He that is without sin cast the first stone." It wasn't about the number of words Jesus spoke or the tone of His voice but it was the way Jesus phrased his sentence. He that is without sin cast the first stone. Every person there who deemed themselves more sanctified than the other quickly became convicted and realized they were sinners or that they had sin in the secret place of their heart. That statement still holds true today. If you really know the heart of God you will resist throwing stones at the downcast and wounded, other wise he that is without sin cast the first stone. Do you know someone that has no sin in his or her life? If so then you are now in heaven.

Stones have many uses and are symbolic of different things throughout the Bible. David use a smooth stone to kill Goliath (I Samuel 17:49), his stone became a weapon. Moses on Mount Sinai received the Ten Commandments by God that were written on stone. We are told that the wells of Abraham and Isaac were filled with stones, which is symbolic of "stopping the flow of the Word in our lives" since the Scripture says, "Out of your most inner part shall flow rivers of Living Water. In this instance the stones are symbolic of the words used by others to destroy your life, ministry, or vision.

Isaiah 54:17, "No weapon that is formed against you shall prosper: and every tongue that shall rise against you in judgment you shall condemn. This is the heritage of the servants of the Lord. And their righteousness is of me saith the Lord." Within this passage there are four points being made that are vital to your success as a Christian. An older Christian man once said that, "Words are like feathers thrown to the wind, once they are released you will never retrieve all of them again. Now if you have ever visited Browning, Montana you would know the power of the wind.

1. No weapon <u>formed against you</u> shall prosper (Why? Because you have authority in Christ Jesus.)
2. Every word spoken against you, <u>condemn it</u> (not the pastor or minister; you)
3. This is your birthright as a child of God (your heritage)
4. Your righteousness comes from The Lord (If God be for you who can be against you?)

The devil is an accuser of the brethren day and night according to Revelation 12:10, let's be honest; the devil hates you and will never be your friend. As long as you are covered in the Blood of Jesus and confess Jesus as Lord, the devil will be out to try and stop you from discovering your destiny in Christ. Sometimes we think God is mad at us or has forgotten about us when trials come our way but contrary to belief God is bragging on you.

Job 1:8, Then the LORD said to Satan, "Have you noticed my servant Job? No one else on earth is like him. He is an honest and innocent man, honoring God and staying away from evil." One tragedy after another swept over Job however, through it all Job did not sin against God or blame God. It is very clear in Job 2:3b the phrase "Without cause" really translates "without sin."

The same is with you concerning the trials and test that have overwhelmed you from time to time and the question of sin. There is even a book entitled "When bad things happen to good people." God had so much confidence in Job that when Satan begin to accuse Job God knew he would continue to serve Him and love Him. The greatest admiration we can pay to God is to serve and worship him all the days of our life.

If you remember soon after the bad reports begin to get around about Job or should I say the gossip, his closest friends came to comfort Job and they did well until their carnal nature got in the way. They should have known the character of Job and his love for God since they were his best friends yet even they begin to think that Job had committed a secret sin and this was the reason for all his troubles. It got to the point that Job just came out and called them "Miserable Comforters" because their words were vain (Job 16:2).

Often when we hear messages about Job it only covers his trial, however trials end and there is a reward to those who hold on and come through. Job 42:12-16 (NIV) says, "The LORD blessed the latter part of Job's life more than the former part. He had fourteen thousand sheep, six thousand camels, a thousand yoke of oxen and a thousand donkeys. ¹³ And he also had seven sons and three daughters. ¹⁴ The first daughter he named Jemimah, the second Keziah and the third Keren-Happuch. ¹⁵ Nowhere in all the land were there found women as beautiful as Job's daughters, and their father granted them an inheritance along with their brothers.

¹⁶ After this, Job lived a hundred and forty years; he saw his children and their children to the fourth generation.

"Tribal Chairman"

Looking back at Genesis 25:22-26, "And the children struggled together within her (Rebecca); and she said, if it be so, why am I thus? And she went to enquire of the Lord. And the Lord said unto her, two nations are in thy womb..." Greatness was about to come forth in Rebecca's life and her question to God was, "Why the struggle?" How many times have we asked God for something in our life only to encounter struggle?

After being elected Chairman of the Blackfeet Nation I begin to struggle concerning what was happening in my life. As Tribal Chairman your life is over whelmed with responsibility and demands. Personal attacks on yourself and family are relentless and that's just from the "church people" notice I didn't say Christian since Christian means to be like Christ and Jesus never threw stones. However you continue to pray, smile, permit the Grace of God to witness through you and every so often minister side by side with those who are doing the talking. Doing what God has called you to do makes people nervous. Stepping out of your comfort zone gets people talking. The young people have a saying, "Don't be hating." As my dad would say, "Walk softly before the Lord Bill." The success of Joseph wasn't that he endured so much hardship, it was that he was willing to forgive whenever offend... if you notice it was his own brothers that cast him into the pit and pronounced that his ministry, existence, and days were over.

I resigned my position with the National Park Service and took a $6,000.00 cut in pay with 100 percent more responsibility. Anyone in their right mind would say that was crazy however, the mind of Christ reasons differently. While we live in the moment, God is looking into the future. My struggle in the present was merely a ripple in the course of God's Plan. I remember telling Muriel (and only Muriel), "What I'm I the preacher or the politician?"

After leaving tribal government I wanted to distance myself as far as possible from anything that was associated with tribal government and tribal issues. My thinking was let somebody else do it. However God doesn't forget, according to the scripture His gifts and calling are without repentance (Romans 11:29). What God gives you he will not take back. I prayed and fasted year after year in the cold of winter for the healing of our land and that God would rise up a leader of courage that would speak for the Blackfeet Nation. Now I wanted to run from that calling that God had placed upon me. He was the one that set me in the Chairman's position just as He had done for kings in the Old Testament.

So I moved to Missoula, Montana and continue with my education at the University of Montana hoping the issue would be resolved. For two years I did not preach, sing, or promote the Gospel...I established myself at Christian Life Center Assembly of God hearing and relearning the Word of God Sunday after Sunday all the while a struggle was stirring in my spirit, "I'm I the preacher or the politician?"

It was during this time I was invited to help with music for a young pastor who was beginning a new work on the Flathead Indian reservation, reluctantly I accepted within a few months I was invited by a friend to minister at a conference he was sponsoring at his church in central Montana. The pastor of the specific church knew nothing of my conversation with Muriel let alone my conversation with God. As I ministered the anointing flowed and many were blessed set free by the power of the Holy Spirit.

As I concluded the message the pastor took the podium and said, "Pastor Old Chief, I have a word from God for you" and then begin to speak over me as I stood about twenty-feet from him. "There is a two-fold anointing in your life. The first is evident by what we have witnessed this night, the other is an "Administrative Anointing" (this I had never heard before) it is an anointing that God has given to you to lead your people, just as Solomon asked for wisdom, God has given you wisdom and called you to lead your people (Blackfeet /Pikuni).

Now this is where the rubber hit the road. You have been struggling in your spirit concerning this calling upon your life. You have even said, "I'm I the preacher or the politician?" That was his exact words. This is when I begin to listen very closely for surely this was the voice of God since this pastor knew nothing about me. Then he went on to say, "You have tried to make them two different issues however God has entwined them as one. As you begin to operate as one the struggle will be over."

At that moment I fell backward without any person touching me except for the Holy Spirit and saw the revelation of what God was doing in my life. When I preached I enjoyed it. When I was speaking for the Blackfeet people I enjoyed it. Yet guilt would overshadow me because I thought it was wrong to serve the people without talking church stuff as the preacher. As I allowed both offices to work together I discovered I became more productive and effective since Jesus is in my life He is going to come forth just the same. Jesus said, "They shall know you by your love." As a Pastor I realized that God had just given me a larger church, and it was no longer behind the four walls of two hymns, a prayer, and see you next Sunday and please bring a side dish.

As I surrendered myself to God's plan I discovered peace and my direction became clear. Doors of opportunity have opened at both levels. I often say, "First and foremost, I'm a minister of the Gospel, called of God to do His work. I don't struggle with my calling...I listen. I obey. I do the best I can to fulfill the task set before me. I now have confidence that the Holy Spirit is leading me. To be in the will of God is pleasing in His sight and it produces success around you.

CHAPTER TWO

Archaeological Christian

In the book of Nahum 1:7, 9b we are reminded of the majesty of God, "The Lord is good, a stronghold in the day of trouble; and he knoweth them that trust him…he will make an utter end: <u>affliction shall not rise up the second time</u>." How many times have you gone through something only to remind God, "Oh no not again!" I thought I was over this. I thought I was past this. I thought I buried this only to have it resurface. At times our past may resemble the living dead…it just won't die.

The scripture in this passage is proclaiming the majesty of God in the times of trouble. He is our stronghold, our fortress, our protection he is a <u>good God</u>! It also assures the Believer that God knows you if you trust him but even more important is the fact that God will bring to an "utter end" to those enemies that will rise up against you. His promise is that, "This ***<u>affliction</u>*** [*trouble*] will not rise up a second time." This is the same trouble as recorded in Psalms 34:6 (NKJV), this poor man cried out, and the LORD heard *him,* and saved him out of <u>all his ***troubles***</u>.

Our life in Christ is about change. From the very moment we come to Jesus and ask Him into our life a transformation begins. At the age of twenty-three I came to Jesus on a Wednesday night after years of self abuse and disappointment…I was that Prodigal Son who had all the riches and comforts before me however, my heart drew toward the world and the things that disillusion our path in life.

I choose to distance myself as far as I could from the God of my childhood. High school became my time of opportunity to cut all ties to Christianity, church, revivals, and yes prayer. As a child the outside of the church was fun, it was a time to join other children as we explored with delight all that nature presented. While the adults sang praises unto God and the Word was preached with enthusiasm and voices of "Amen" filled the air.

As children we just played, giggled, and ran wildly throughout the evening every once in a while peeking our heads through the door waiting for the moment when the music started and all the people would begin to dance in the Spirit from one side of the large tent to the other. It was fun since most services lasted well past the mid-night hour and when you are nine and ten years old this is a kid's paradise.

Soon I discovered there was responsibilities required of my siblings and me as we begin to grow. Church became confined, restricted, and miserable, as we were required to attend and set through each service. I often wondered how we learned anything as a child since most adults appeared confused and bewildered by what they heard.

To be honest what I did retain about Jesus came from my mother as she prayed with us at our bedside. Often she would read Bible stories to us about David, Samson, Joshua, and of course Jesus. I frequently heard my dad-praying hour after hour late into the night just down the hallway. These are the lessons that were embedded into my spirit as a child.

There were no Sunday school classes or youth services or children's services in those old Indian Campmeetings…you just showed-up and learned what the adults learned and everyone pretend to be learning and growing in the Lord as they put it. If you got lost during the message you just shouted, "Amen…preach it brother" and others followed.

I guess that's why later there was confusion about doctrine, about men's hair length, and makeup, women wearing dresses verse pants, Christmas, Easter, watching television, going to movies, or listening to the radio, Indian days, rodeos, sporting events, you name it there was a fight over it. There was more fighting in the church than in a bar room on Saturday night. According to the adults, everything was of the devil. Well as they say times have changed.

I am not saying the church was full of hypocrites; I was just in a season of transition. I was looking for the truth as I matured into a young man. In spite of everything I honored my parents who were Evangelist and Pastors of *Victory Outreach* in Browning, Montana a former run down "stick-game" house that they converted into a cozy church. I'd like to think that old gambling house just got saved. Whenever I was called upon to assist them in church activities I would do my best, then quickly disappear. I guess my problem was that I loved my parents but dislike the church in general.

My brother Gayle and I joined high school rodeo because of the travel opportunities throughout the state of Montana, what we discovered was we were "good cowboys" and always up for the challenge. When we weren't riding for the school we would stay on local ranches and ride their stock just for the excitement. Places like "Hells Half Acre, Two Medicine, just below the Old Mission, Babb, and Durham on the Black Weasel and Still Smoking ranches. These are places only other Blackfeet will recognize.

It was during our high school rodeo days I often felt resentful because our parents never attended one event to support us. As a young man I would look throughout the crowd in hopes of seeing their faces, for a brief moment excitement would fill my heart however this was always short lived and I would continue to focus on what I was doing and that entailed riding bulls and bareback horses.

Later in life my son Billy Dean played basketball for the Browning High School and I would attend his games. One time I walked into my dad's home to find him listening to KSEN radio as my son's name was mentioned again and again going up and down the court. I told my dad, "Let me take you to one of his home games" and his reply was, "I can't go…I have set a standard too high in my life and the sad part it isn't even a Biblical standard, it's a man-made standard." Never have I felt as sad for an individual as

I did for my dad. I turned and went out the door as he continued to listen for his grandson's name on the radio.

The Bible tells us that the devil is an "accuser of the brethren" Satan is out to steal, kill, and destroy. His assignment is to keep you from serving God and fulfilling your destiny. God had a calling upon my life and I often wonder what it would have been like if I had continued to serve Jesus throughout my youth. However, I realize you can't live your life over but you can live it different.

It's situations like this that ensnare individuals into a spiritual bondage. They become that "Archaeological Christian" who is always trying to relive the past hoping they can change the outcome some how. An archaeologist is a person who digs up the past and studies ancient people's lifestyle. Recently my brother and I talked about our childhood past with much humor and there is no resentment concerning our up bringing. Those experiences were reality; they helped shape and develop our character.

I often encounter Christian people who continue to relive their past. Past hurts, past failures, past disappointments, a product of their bitterness. The scripture declares "You shall know them by their fruit." What type of fruit are you producing? I don't want my children or grandchildren living my mistakes. I don't want them to be fighting my old battles but if I fill their spirit with my old garbage from the past it will soon influence them, just as it did me. I have decided to follow Jesus and put my past under the blood.

As a parent it is my responsibility to inspire, lead, and protect my family, and the best way to accomplish the task is learn from my mistakes…to be honest and ask guidance from others and the Holy Spirit. Our world consists of knowledge at every level, so there is no excuse for ignorance in this day and age.

The very first thing that happened in Jacob's life after his encounter with God in Genesis 32 was "Reconciliation" with his brother Esau. Proverbs 16:7 says, *"When a man's ways please the Lord, he maketh even his enemies to be at peace with him."* Jacob reconciled with God at a place he later called "Penile" (I have seen God face to face). Then reconciliation begins with others. One factor we must remember is that it is often easier to forgive others, than to for give ourselves.

Reconciliation is more than having someone wash your feet and say they are sorry for past generational sins, it is having access to the "Mercy-Seat of God" through Jesus Christ, in His death on the Cross by the shedding of His blood in His vivid sacrifice for sin, by which God shows mercy to sinners. Many of our troubles [affliction] stem from digging up the past or reliving traumatic moments in the videotape (DVD/smartphone) of our mind.

A face-to-face encounter with God will change the very atmosphere of your entire life. Your very appearance will be altered, your peace will be re-establish, your joy will be restored…*God will make even your enemies to be at peace with you.* When trouble comes, we are often drawn to our knees in prayer, which gets us ready for the unknown. Once again God reminds Jacob in Genesis 35:10 that his name will no longer be Jacob but Israel and proclaims the promises that will overtake him.

Genesis 35:11-15 (New International Version)
And God said to him, "I am God Almighty (El-Shaddai); be
fruitful and increase in number. A nation and a community of
nations will come from you, and kings will come from your
body. [12] The land I gave to Abraham and Isaac I also give to
you, and I will give this land to your descendants after you."
[13] Then God went up from him at the place where he had
talked with him. [14] Jacob set up a stone pillar at the place
<u>where God had talked with him</u>, and he poured out a drink
offering on it; he also poured oil on it. [15] Jacob called the place
where God had talked with him <u>Bethel</u> {House of God}.

The Secret Place

- Great victories come because of great battles
- Great testimonies come because of great trials

Psalm 91:1 & 4, "He who dwells in the *(secret place)* of the Most
High will rest in the shadow of the Almighty. He will cover you
with his feathers, and under his wings you will find refuge…"

Where do you go to find God?

Despite every attack, threat and fear, God will victoriously
liberate your spirit and bring you into a deeper relationship with
Him. From walking with the dead, to restoring the heart…*the
heart is the life source of man*. Only God can make known the "true
heart of a person."

Regardless of the severity of any trial, despite how heavy trouble weighs in on life's scale, one thing is certain: you will survive - and begin again. God will not allow you to go through anything that you're not able to bear (endure). II Corinthians 10:13, "There hath no temptation taken you but such is common to man: but God is faithful, (NIV) he will not let you be tempted beyond what you can bear. But *when you are tempted, he will also provide a way out so that you can stand up under it*."

Psalms 23:5-6 NIV,
You prepare a table before me in the presence of my enemies
You anoint my head with oil (a sign that
a person is dedicated to God)
My cup overflows
Surely goodness and mercy shall follow
me all the days of my life
And I will dwell in the house of the Lord forever.

David penned these words in Psalms 51:4, 10-12, & 17: Against thee, thee only, have I sinned, and done this evil in thy sight... Create in me a clean heart, O God; and renew a right spirit within me. Cast me not away from thy presence; and take not thy holy spirit from me. Restore unto me the joy of thy Salvation; and uphold me with thy free spirit."

Some year's back I was driving down the road and I realized I had let the devil steal my joy, without joy we can't laugh or smile. That evening as Muriel and I talked I told her, "I don't smile or laugh any more." She said I know, I was just wondering how long it would be before you noticed. That is a horrible thought since

I am a person who loves to laugh and most often will smile at you (for those wondering my teeth are real). The Word of God declares that the, "Joy of the Lord is my strength." So when you come down to it joy is more than a smile or laughter it is where my strength comes from.

There are times we become weary in well doing. In other words we become tired and burned out because we become too churched. I had a pastor friend once tell me in one of my _busier than thou moments_, "Bill! Jesus died for the Church, you don't have to." And that has stayed with me all these years. As ministers we try to become everything to the church thinking if we don't do it, it won't get done. In the smaller Indian reservation churches the pastor is the song leader, preacher, plummer, carpenter, office staff, counselor, youth leader, men's and women's leader, and childcare attendant. Then they wonder why most pastors don't last on the reservation.

These three steps focus our direction toward God & establish our priorities

1. **Solitude:** spending time alone with God
2. **Prayer:** speaking with God [is offering to God petitions or requests for mercies desired and thanksgiving and praise for blessings received…at times stop talking and listen as God speaks into you, conversation is a two way street]
3. **Deposit God's Word** in your spirit: preparing for the challenges that are yet to come

"When we deal with problems or issues in our lives, we must go to the root or the source of that specific problem."

- **Physical abuse is a problem…what is the source?**
- **Drug abuse is a problem…what is the source?**
- **Alcohol is a problem…what is the source?**
- **Sexual abuse is a problem…what is the source?**

It doesn't matter how many treatment centers are built on the reservations or in our communities, genuine change will never happen until we deal with the root of the problem. Alcohol is not a physical problem; it's a spiritual problem. What happens in the spiritual realm affects the natural realm. Romans 8:22, *"We know that the whole creation has been groaning as in the pains of childbirth right up to the present time."* What Adam did in the flesh by sinning caused all of creation to suffer. <u>When we cover up the problem, it continues to manifest.</u> No wonder why in England they call alcohol "spirits" some believe that you gain someone else's spirit when you drink alcohol.

Sin will destroy a vision, a ministry, a family…a person if gone unchecked "Living in the past will cripple your dreams, visions…your purpose"

There is a song I have written and recorded that I sing at most services as I travel, it is a worship song but it speaks to the spirit of man since it says, *"Jesus it's me I'm coming on bended knees. Jesus it's me take these chains from my life and set me free. My heart cries out to be free…Jesus it's me."* In those moments of brokenness God will speak to you, in those seasons you are crushed only God can put back the pieces of your life. For if I am broken I have the ability to pick up the pieces however, if I am crushed only God can restore me, only God can heal what is crushed. Psalm 34:18 (New Living Translation) *the Lord is close to the <u>brokenhearted</u>; he rescues those whose spirits are <u>crushed</u>.*

CHAPTER THREE

Commodity Cheese Ministry

Sometime after hurricane Katrina had devastated the New Orleans area I was asked to do consultation for the Blackfeet Tribe in a number of the Parishes including St. Bernard and Gretna that were damaged the most by the hurricane. My mission was to assist other tribal officials and establish a plan of recovery and employment involving the Blackfeet Nation's large number of seasonal fire fighters. This project took us to New Orleans a number of times and allowed us to build relationships with the local government leaders.

It was during this time that a mayor (I won't mention any names) invited us to lunch for a traditional "Cajun meal" in the Parish of Gretna. Coming from the north I really didn't know what to expect. Visions of frog legs, alligator, crawfish, and possum filled my mind but to my dismay we were served "beans with rice" with a little barbeque pork and hush puppies on the side with iced tea. After a few moments the mayor asked, "What do you think?" He then went on to say this type of meal was common in the early days since it was a "poor man's" food now it was chic' to be served in the restaurants throughout Louisiana.

Not wanting to pop the honorable mayor's bubble I turned to a Blackfeet Tribal Council member and said, "We grew up on beans and rice…I didn't know it was a poor man's food?" We just laughed and continued to enjoy our exotic Cajun dish without the alligator, or the frog legs, or the possum.

What the mayor didn't realize was beans and rice was food given to the Blackfeet Indians through the "Commodity Food Distribution Program" and the best part of the package was the canned chopped meat that we would fry and stick between Indian bannock bread not forgetting to add a big thick slice of commodity cheese from the five pound loaf marked, "Product of U.S. Government."

I never did learn how to fry the powdered eggs or get used to the countless boxes of dried raisins. Well the government may have taken everything from us, but thank Uncle Sam for that cheese… it helped ease the pain somewhat. As a matter of fact, I didn't know cheese came in individual slices until my teens. Talk about cultural shock.

Today there are those on Christian television that promote their 'commodity cheese' days as a ministry starter. They recall the days of cheese from the government and food stamps as the worst times of their lives. Well, again I have no regrets, anger, or bitterness about my past and growing up on 'commodities' I like to think the body I have today was because of those good old commodities. Somebody say Amen! Without commodities we would not have present day "Fry Bread Queens."

During this time of youth we as children played as long as the late northern Montana summer sunlight would last before setting, which was around 10:30 or 11:00 p.m. in between that period of time we would often become hungry and like Esau of old we were willing to sell our birthright for a quick meal. Just down the street from my grandparents house (we live next door to them) was an older widow lady that had a unique gift from the Creator to bake the most desirable bread.

Like a cowboy throwing a rope around a running calf and stopping it suddenly, our noses would catch a whiff of her bread cooling through her open windows and we would stop in our tracks, the aroma was indescribable. The next step was how to obtain some without looking like we were little beggars. In her devout way and grandmother nature she would call us to her back porch with a special pan prepared just for us...the "Willow Creek Kids." Our world ended at Seventy-Five Cent Hole, which was our best swimming hole about a mile from our house. Today as an adult I understand I can step over it.

I have tasted other bread since that time but nothing can duplicate the golden brown crust as the warm butter flowed gently downward, or the sweetness that captured every taste bud your mind could cultivate, and the tenderness of the inside as you took your first bite...all one could do was close your eyes, roll you head backward and enjoy the moment.

Her bread is what David described when he said, "*O, taste and see that the Lord is good: blessed is the man that trusteth in Him* (Psalms 34:6)." My life in Christ has been one of great appreciation.

Before Jesus came into my life I was just another person surviving from day to day. Really that is all we do.

Most families live from paycheck to pay check never able to fulfill their dreams or basic desires. They're always promising themselves that tomorrow is going to be better. Yet in our own strengths and abilities we'll constantly be in need of a better job, a bigger house, a newer car, or another relationship.

According to one statistic concerning Montana Native American males I should have either died at a young age or have been housed in the federal prison for the rest of my life and looking back to those I hung out with or went to high school with that statement was true. Most of those who called me friend during my "Prodigal Son" years have since withered away in societies prisons, graves, or live a life of obscurity.

"Ministry Opportunities"

Sometime back I was ministering and the Holy Spirit quickened me with this phrase; "<u>Missing Your Season of Opportunity</u>..."

- Because of unbelief
- Priorities in your life
- Or plain old disobedience

Within the scriptures there are examples of numbers having significant implication, for example the number eight is symbolic of "New Beginnings & Restoration." Sometime back when I entered into the year 2008 during a New Years Eve service as I ministered, I believed God was going to do something new and fresh in my life, in my ministry, in my future. Thus 2008 became a "NEW Season or Appointed Time" for me…I accepted it as a word form the Lord, I anticipated it to happen.

What happen in 2007 was past history. It was gone…I couldn't reclaim the events of '07 even if I wanted to. Seven is a number of completeness or perfection…I may have not succeed in 2007, but I didn't have to fail in 2008…it was time to take back what the enemy had stolen from me. I could continue living my life as before, hoping tomorrow would get better, hoping I would win the lotto even though I don't gamble, or hoping some rich stranger would die and put me in their will. I choose to accept the word of the Lord. What is God doing now? It doesn't matter if its 2015 or 2025 God is able to meet me in the present. If God has called me He will equip me concerning the ministry.

2012 became another pivotal year as the Holy Spirit revealed to me that the number twelve is symbolic of "Divine Government." If you look at it from the individual perspective you will conclude what does that have to do in my mundane life however, as the spirit of revelation opens interpretation you begin to realize that God is taking you into a great blessing. The number eleven is a symbolic of confusion, chaos, and disorder, which it was throughout most of the world during 2011. One example is the great tidal wave that hit Japan because of a 9.0 earthquake killing many and relocation the entire nation of Japan 8 feet closer to the United States.

2012 became a period of anticipation for something better, something greater in the spirit realm. A hunger arisen within me that I thought was gone and that was a hunger for the things of God. The scripture instructs us to "seek ye first the kingdom of God and His righteousness and all these things shall be added to you." I want God to restore divine government back into my life. I want to be part of His great plan in this hour and not just in the sweet by and by.

Regarding every decision we make there is consequences, it is the ripple effect I mention earlier that our lives affect at least twenty others whether we do good or bad. The Bible tells us in II Corinthians 5:17, "Therefore, if anyone *is* in Christ, *he is* a new creation; old things have passed away; behold, all things have become new." We are instructed to live by faith or as the scripture puts it, *"The just shall live by faith."*

Faith is a verb, meaning it portrays or expresses ACTION…you have to do something with faith in order for faith to work. How many times have you heard that God is not moved by our feelings, He is moved by our faith in Him. If you want to experience your faith in action do something you've never done before…like laying your hands on the sick and watch what God will do. Step out of your comfort zone and experience the reality of God's Word in your everyday actives. *"And from the days of John the Baptist until now the kingdom of heaven suffereth violence, and the violent take it by force."*

You licked your proverbial wounds, you shed your tears, and you felt sorry for yourself…now it's time to rise up in the power of the Holy Ghost. God declares, "So I will restore/repay to you the years that the swarming locust has eaten, the crawling locust, the consuming locust, and the chewing locust…(Joel 2:25). Years:

meaning the "Times & Seasons" of your life or the blessings that were Stolen.

"I long to see you so that I may <u>impart</u> to you some spiritual gift to make you strong"— (Romans 1:11). Paul is speaking of the "Gift of divine GRACE" translated, unmerited favor. It is something we don't deserve yet God gives to us freely. It is important that we do the same to others that may be having difficulties in serving God; we must show it by;

- Imparting words of encouragement
- Build, rather than tear down
- Pray, rather than gossip
- Love, rather than hate…

Building People, not judging them!

Preaching hope and grace produces greater results in people.

1. Your Ministry Goal should be to build people by the <u>Grace of God</u>.
2. Some come with broken hearts, destroyed by the sin of the world
3. Others are discouraged because of the many failures they have encountered in their life
4. Still, others are just tired of running from God and need a SAVIOR…a resting place

Serve God or Serve the World

I Kings 18:21, "And Elijah came unto all the people, and said, how long halt ye between <u>two opinions</u> (thoughts which divide &

distract the mind)? If the LORD be God, follow him: but if Baal, then follow him. And the people answered him not a word." (New Life Version Bible)...Elijah came near all the people and said, "How long will you be divided between <u>two ways of thinking</u>? "*A double minded man is unstable in all his ways (James 1:8)*."

<u>No Looking Back</u> (Get your mind made-up to serve the Lord)

- An ungodly person will tell you it's alright to "sin a little," get even, get mad, quit, give up, distort the truth or just stop trying
- There is no such thing as a little sin. (1/3 of the angels were cast out of heaven because of sin) Revelation 12:4~Isaiah 14:12

Ministry has many rewards to offer and yes there are disappointments also. Ministry is more than handing out Bible tracks on a Friday evening or serving refreshments to the needy. Ministry isn't even about a building; it's about changing and building lives that have been wrecked because of sin. Sin recovery takes time, it takes love, and it takes the Word of God since Romans 12:2 says, "*And be not conformed to this world: but be ye transformed by the renewing of your mind...*"

Birthing your ministry, where do you begin?

Prayer is communicating with God! But more than just "talking to God, "prayer involves our relationship with God. As in any relationship, sometimes we talk, sometimes we listen, and sometimes we just enjoy being together. Our Heavenly Father teaches us to "pray without ceasing" also, we must listen with our heart since He speaks in a *"still small voice."* (I Kings 19:12)

As a Teacher I developed a training manual entitled: *"Visionary Leadership Development Principles"*: to identify, develop, educate, and equip future leaders…that will transform their lives, community, and world through Christ Jesus.

1. Identify (Recognize the leader in you)
2. Develop (Develop or educate the leader in you)
3. Equip (unearth your potential as a leader…see the potential in you)
4. Implementing Process (Transform your world with hands on experience…quit waiting, start doing)

Prayers Make a Difference

The disciple asked Jesus one day, "Lord, teach us to pray."

Our Father which art in heaven, Hallow (sacred) be thy name. Thy kingdom come. Thy will be done, as in heaven, so in earth. Give us this day our <u>daily bread</u>. And forgive us our sins; for we also forgive every one that is indebted to us. And lead us not into temptation; but deliver us from evil. (Luke 11:1)

> I heard a man once say, *"Our prayers may be awkward. Our attempts may be feeble. But since the power of prayer is in the one who hears it and not the one who says it, our prayers do make a difference."*

The Prayer Ministry of "Visionary Leadership Development" is <u>Prayer Warriors</u> who intercede in prayer for the needs of others, the church and our nation. There isn't a week that goes by that my wife and I aren't called upon to pray for those who may be in the hospital, in their homes, or in the ministry. James 5:16b, says, "The effectual fervent prayer (prayer with zeal, holy, just, innocent) of a righteous man availeth much."

How ministries are birthed

- It is in time's of prayer that God begins to speak to your spirit and reveals His intent for your life
- Prayer produces compassion for the lost
- Prayer provides guidance through the Holy Spirit

Prayer humbles us before God...prayer prepares us for the unknown

> "All men dream: but not equally. Those who dream by
> night in the dusty recesses of their minds wake in the
> day to find that it was vanity: but the <u>dreamers of the
> day</u> are dangerous men, for they may act their dream
> with open eyes to make it possible." T.E. Lawrence
> Watch your thoughts. They become words.
> Watch your words, they become actions.
> Watch your actions, they become habits.
> Watch your habits, they become character.
> Watch your character, they become your destiny.
> Pastor C. T.

The following statements are words that will enhance the vision of your calling, and your ministry. It is true that each great journey begins with one step. During my second year as a Christian, what they call being a "Babe in the Lord" I was asked by my Pastor Johnny Iron Shirt to help him in revival meetings on the Fort Peck and Fort Belknap Indian Reservations located in northeastern Montana.

As we traveled back to Browning, in the dark of the night just a few miles out of Shelby he turned to me after our praying for many miles and said, "Bill, one of these days you will be the one traveling down the road from a revival meeting. You will be taking other young men with you sharing the Gospel." At the moment my mind (faith) couldn't comprehend what the Lord was speaking from his spirit into mine. I didn't sing or preach in those early years and when I did testify before the church congregation I cried like a baby every time, which embarrassed me greatly since I was still a young man, tall, strong, and Blackfeet (Pikuni).

This word would be fulfilled later in my life and I would be speaking the same into other young men who had traveled with me. Jesus said he would make us 'fishers of men.'

- You don't need huge financial sums to begin your ministry
- You don't need to be ordained
- You don't need to be incorporated

You do need approval by God, vision, purpose, & direction.

Vision is produced in times of prayer. Direction is given from the Holy Spirit, it is what provides the purpose or motive concerning your calling into the ministry. "I was hungry and you gave me something to eat, I was thirsty and you gave me something to drink, I was a stranger and you invited me in, I needed cloths and you clothed me, I was sick, and you visited me: I was in prison and you came to visit me." (Matthew 25:35 NIV)

Ministry is "The Act of Serving Others" <u>Leadership</u> is defined as envisioning a better future for yourself, the job at hand, and those with whom you labor. "But we will give ourselves <u>continually to prayer</u>, and to the <u>ministry</u> (a servant) of the Word." (Acts 6:4)

This text is telling us that 'prayer' is more important than 'preaching'…since it is mentioned first. Without a proper prayer life, there can be no proper ministry. <u>Ministry is birthed out of prayer</u>, prayer produces vision! Prayer that produces mighty ministries becomes effective for the kingdom of God because of the divine results.

Ministry can be entered at different levels

The Bible tells us Jesus was 12 years old when he taught in the temple, in other words Jesus entered into the ministry at 12 years of age. He later went fulltime when he turned thirty years old. Listed are examples of ministry stages that I have functioned in one time or another. In this example you may see yourself also.

- o Short term: Ministry Leadership Development Principles is a short term course that we have developed to build-up and instruct potential church leaders at all levels. The condensed course could be done in a weekend and the full course takes about five months.

○ Long term: commitment to God, to your family to your calling

○ Existing programs: within the church which could be new & creative ministries that reach a specific group of people if just for a season…there is no time limit on this type of ministry such as ministering to the street people, elderly visitations, community outreaches, musician, greeter at the door or prayer warrior.

1. If you desire to fulfill a ministry need, talk with your Pastor…seek council with the ministry team leader or godly advisors within your church.
2. Inquire how the local church or believers can assist your efforts…be creative yet flexible, allow the Holy Spirit to lead you.
3. Once you put your hands to the plow, stay committed, focused, & faithful until the task is completed…never push off on another, what God has called you to do.

Most of all let Jesus be exalted by your obedience. *To whom much is given, mush is required.* These words speak for them self; they express responsibility for those who desire leadership or ministry position. As we are reminded in the book of Psalms75:7, "Promotion comes from God." The problem with most immature people is they seek 'self-promotion' rather than promotion from God. I would rather have God open the door and present the assignment to me than someone I have deceived into believing I'm ready for the unknown.

I heard a minister from the southwest who had found his way to Browning in the coldness of winter describe his desire to minister like his pastor. As a young Christian he was full of zeal but no wisdom. Zeal without wisdom is like a baby with a load gun…it could go off at any moment.

This young man would witness the power of God in his pastor's life, he would see the Spirit of God moving in the services and even the attention the pastor was receiving, this intrigued him to the point of wanting what his pastor had in his life. On a hot summer evening he located his pastor sitting in the front yard of his home drinking iced tea under the shade of a tree.

Pastor! "I want a double portion of what you have he announced." The pastor in his wisdom replied, "No you don't." After going around and around the pastor finally agreed he would pray for this young 'foolish' man. It wasn't long after this that the pastor noticed a battle weary, beaten down, disappointed person coming his way near the shaded area that he spent time under during the heat of the day.

Pastor! Pray for me, the devil is doing this to me and the devil is doing that to me. The glamour and glory of what he had seen just weeks before was short lived as the realization of, *"To whom much is given, much is required."* I never sought the attention of a platform ministry because in a way I'm somewhat backward. I just don't go up to people and start talking as if we were old friends. My nature is to be alone in the comfort of my home…I don't even like answering the phone. Sometimes my shyness maybe taken for arrogance but I'm a friendly person once you get to know me.

When we came to Jesus my wife and I took it upon ourselves to clean the church after each meeting it wasn't because we had nothing to do, on the contrary we had busy lives from sun-up to sun down. There wasn't anyone else doing it and we just filled in a void that lasted a couple of years. Often after revivals we would get home well past 2:00 a.m. only to awaken by the alarm around 5:30 a.m. to begin our day.

Those days of cleaning the dirty restrooms and vacuum the large church floor, then taking out all the trash made me appreciate the days that followed as our 'gift made room for us." Your not always going to be in a "spiritual prison" like Joseph was. God is getting you ready for the palace. You might think being a Sunday school teacher is your prison but God is allowing you to pour into his precious children golden nuggets that will help them later in life.

Joshua ministered 40 years to Moses and the word minister isn't talking about living in luxury hotels, jet setting across the country in private jets and then eating in the finest restaurants. It meant waiting on Moses as duty called. That may entail ministering in a non- glamorous position. It's not about carrying the ministers Bible and serving water every once in a while either.

I went from the restroom to the throne room ministering the Word of God again and again. Since then I have had the opportunity to minister before hundreds and at one point 65,000 men during a Promise Keepers conference in Seattle, Washington. You will never know how God will use you but first you must be useable. My prayer has always been, "Lord send me where the people are hungry for you."

When I was ordained in our local church I felt so insignificant because I realized what was about to happen would change my life forever. As an ordained minister I was proclaiming to my community and the world that Jesus was first and foremost in my life. My prayer was the same as Solomon who became the third king of Israel and reigned 40 years: I Kings 3:9-12, "Give me an understanding heart to judge thy people." What Solomon was asking for was wisdom! Later in life Solomon wrote these words in Proverbs 4:5, 7, "Get wisdom, get understanding. Wisdom is the principal thing; therefore get wisdom: and with all thy getting get understanding."

The shortest scripture in the Bible is found in John 11:35, "Jesus wept." As a minister I must take on the character of Christ. I can't separate Christ from my Christian walk…they are one in the same. I don't cloth myself with Jesus on Sunday morning and then live my life any way I want the rest of the week. The very core of Jesus was to love others. He went a step further and said, "But I say unto you, Love your enemies, bless them that curse you, do good to them that hate you, and pray for them which despitefully use you, and persecute you; that you may be the children of your Father…" (Matthew 5:44-45a)

CHAPTER FOUR

Vision

In the early days of my conversion, I wasn't taught about 'vision' or was it a principle that was acted upon. Our small church in Browning was about salvation by faith. We danced, we shouted, we prayed, evil spirits were cast out, we gave offerings and tithe, we even had visiting ministers but we didn't talk about the importance of VISION.

Our objective was to wait for the Rapture of the Church and everything else would fall into place. The Bible says, "_Where there is no vision, the people will parish_ (die)..." I envision spiritual death worst than a natural death since _to be absent from the body is to present with the Lord however_, to be spiritual dead is bondage and oppression in the flesh here on earth. You can feel it, taste it suffer in it day after day. It is a decaying stench that follows you constantly.

So service after service I went just because I thought it was the right thing to do. That's what you do after you get saved isn't'? You find a local church to attend for the rest of your life and then one day they bury you and say what a good person you were for being faithful (loyal) to the church. You didn't rock the boat, you didn't ask funny question that would embarrass the leadership. You simply obeyed and gave and gave and gave.

What I discovered is that there is a greater command that Jesus left for us and that is found in Mark 16: 15-18, 20 NKJV, "And He said to them, "Go into all the world and preach the gospel to every creature. He who believes and is baptized will be saved; but he who does not believe will be condemned. <u>And these signs will follow those who believe</u>: In My name they will cast out demons; they will speak with new tongues; they will take up serpents; and if they drink anything deadly, it will by no means hurt them; <u>they will lay hands on the sick, and they will recover</u>. And they went out and preached everywhere, the Lord working with *them* and confirming the word through the accompanying signs. Amen.""

What I've come to learn is not everyone can handle vision, since it implies change. Godly vision can play havoc with a church, it makes leaders nervous…people start getting healed, delivered, set-free, the people start growing in the knowledge of Jesus Christ.

They begin to see the possibilities and the light at the end of the tunnel rather than perpetual darkness of ignorance. Paul in 1 Co. 13:11 said, "When I was a child, I spoke as a child, I understood as a child: <u>but when I became a man</u>, I put away childish things."

God spoke to Israel in visions, which gave instructions, comfort, and promises (Genesis 46:2). The very first thing Jesus instilled into his disciples {Peter & Andrew} was VISION (Matthew 4:19).

"Follow Me, and <u>I will make you fishers of men</u>." Vision without purpose is meaningless.

Habakkuk 2:2-3 (New Century Version)
[2] The LORD answered me:
"Write down the vision; write it clearly on clay tablets
so whoever reads it can run to tell others.
[3] It is not yet time for the message to come true,
but that time is coming soon; the message will come true.
It may seem like a long time, but be patient and wait for it,
because it will surely come;
it will not be delayed."

- Your vision must have purpose: When we designed *Ministry Leadership Development Principles* it was for the sole purpose of identifying, building-up and equipping ministry leaders, there was a beginning and an end. We didn't have to guess about the outcome because we had written the vision down and made it plain for all to understand.
- Your vision must be strong enough to motivate you into action: 2001 was the year I returned back to the University of Montana to complete my Bachelor's Degree. All my children had graduated from high school, now it was my turn to complete what I had begun years before. It was difficult since I was a "non-traditional student" and the biggest enemy was my pride, "What would people think of this old man going to the university with kids half his age?" However, in the back of my mind I was reminded that I was the first in my entire family to obtain a college degree (A.A. Degree from the Blackfeet Community College)

and this was just another part of my educational journey. Also I felt it was my responsibility to remain a positive roll model for my family and others that would follow. A vision is a purpose for life: that's strong enough to motivate you every day. Real enough, to stir you to action. The Bible says it this way, "Call those things which are not as if they are." Wow! You'll hear me quote that from time to time, allow the Word into your heart.

Vision: is the ability to perceive something as through mental acuteness (Webster's dictionary)

- Vision is more than a moment of thought that is called daydreaming
- Vision is the ability to turn a dream into reality (this book is a product of a vision, now reality since you are reading what was once in my mind / heart)
- Vision is within the spirit of a person. The only way you can destroy the vision is to destroy the person.

Often we confuse leadership with vision. Leadership can be learned from developing outward sources whereas vision is birth within as a seed. Leadership is the capacity to translate VISION into reality. Leadership <u>is not</u> exerting authority ~ its empowering people…giving them the tools they need to do the job. God Himself calls us to leadership…He is the ultimate leader. "…*When thou art converted, strengthen thy brethren*" (Luke 22:32). One example of excellent learned leadership skills is the United States Marine Corps who produce countless leaders, my two sons included.

The principle of vision has completely changed {transformed} my life. How can I strengthen my brother if I'm weak? How can I speak deliverance into a person if I'm bound and oppressed? How can I speak about the 8810 (7487 belong to you) promises of God, which include financial blessings if I'm broke and living in poverty?

This very book is a product of vision. Someone planted the seed another watered but God gave the increase. They encouraged me to write. After sometime I believed I could actually put down in words what was in my heart. What was in my mind became reality or tangible…but it required research, dedication, and the will to follow through to the conclusion. Romans 4:17b, "Call those thing which be not as though they were."

Over the years I learned by teaching *"Ministry Leadership Development Principles:"* to design a foundation, build a structure, and implement the principles learned by developing a <u>leadership blueprint</u> that can be successfully completed within a specific time period. Again I use this book as an example, if I didn't complete it in a specific time frame I would be writing the rest of my life and no one would benefit from it. Do what God has called you to <u>do with excellence</u>. We often complain in the church that young people are drawn away by the world…well look how the world presents itself they are the Hummer and the church is the Moped.

Visionary Leadership (Defined)

Enabling a group to engage together in the process of developing, sharing, and moving into vision, <u>and then living it out</u>.

- We begin with a thought (Is it really possible to write a book?) What was holding me down was my environment. I'm an Indian living on a reservation where unemployment is double digits. What do I have to say that others would want to listen too? It was only after realizing God has gifted me. Changed me and given me a future beyond the Blackfeet Indian reservation.
- Change or transformation is the end results of vision. (What was in my heart is now tangible it became a reality)
- Vision motivated the change factor… producing a 'blueprint' to build upon.
- Therefore a plan specifically designed was created which resulted in "Some Where in Montana" A Spiritual Awakening in Blackfeet Country.

Leadership with Vision:

1. Requires stepping outside of your **comfort zone**…you will offend people who find it un-necessary to change the status quo. Do you realize there are people who sleep until 12:00 or 1:00 p.m. everyday? They don't want change, then there are others who just want to hang out day after day their vision is short term guided by an emotional whim.
2. If you can accomplish the task or vision on your own, and you don't need the help of God, it is a good indicator you are operating in your **comfort zone**. Utilizing your own gifting and abilities which moves God out of the equation. He is a jealous God and wants all the glory. As we prepared to publish this book, packets of a partial manuscript were sent out to individuals, believing they would catch the

vision and become part of the fulfillment of the vision...
some did, others may have tossed it aside thinking it a
foolish dream. I like to call it the "Joseph Syndrome" the
vision is just too colorful for some to except (Genesis
37:5). However a true vision will be completed because
of God...He will see it through. He will be glorified and
lifted up. <u>In reality the vision is the property of God</u>.

<u>Bridging the Gap</u> "Transforming knowledge into everyday
practical use. How do you take from the classroom or church
house to the real world?" This is often the problem with the things
we learn. Often an individual will say when it involves math in the
classroom, "Where and when will I ever use this?" As Christian
leaders it is important to be informed concerning all aspects of
leadership skills including:

- Financial concepts, basic economics
- Mentoring styles
- Marketing strategies: Product, Price, Place, and Promotion
- SWOT analysis: **S**trengths, **W**eaknesses, **O**pportunities,
  and **T**hreats
- Communicating and public speaking
- Defining your vision, staying up to date on current events
  that are shaping the world
- Developing your leadership skills to the next level

Many Christian leaders deem it unnecessary to study anything
beyond the Bible but if you take into account the disciples who
later were promoted to Apostles they were educated men who
were entrepreneurs, business leaders, accountants, medical

providers, skilled in the law as well as students of the Torah, which is the first five books of the Old Testament or the book of Moses. This is the tradition of the Jewish culture to be skilled and diversified in order to succeed in the world.

1 Corinthians 14:38, *"But if a man be <u>ignorant</u>, let him <u>be ignorant</u>* {unlearned, not know or unable to understand}." I have a business license with the Blackfeet Nation for "Old Chief Consultants" our business that was birth after serving as Blackfeet Tribal Chairman and as a consultant in tribal and political matters I have had the opportunity to part take in major business ventures within and beyond the Blackfeet Indian reservation that have bettered the lives of many.

Some pastors have small churches because their vision is small…a larger congregation means more responsibility. They never see the possibilities, only the problems and this cripples their vision of reaching the community for Jesus. I once heard a person say, "We don't want a large church, this is a family church and we want to keep it that way." That self-proclaimed prophecy is a reality today. Except for a few family members, the church fractioned as a wake and funeral center serving the needs of the dead. Today the church doors are closed because there was no vision!

That is the same reason some people are never promoted on the job because they think more money equals paying higher taxes. Their thinking becomes stagnated, their vision deformed, and their outlook gloomy. The Bible says, "That God has laid up the wealth of the wicked for the righteous" what are you going to do when your payday comes, reject it because you think money is evil? The text says, "For the <u>love</u> of money is the root of all evil" not money in itself. Do you see the difference? (I Timothy 6:10)

Sometime back the Holy Spirit prompted me to buy a car for an elder lady who was without. So I went to the car lot and choose the best vehicle there. After driving the car into her drive way I knocked on the door and announced to her what I had done. Her first response was, "I can't have that in my name they'll cut me off Social Security!" I had just paid thousands of dollars in cash for a beautiful car that a person didn't want because her vision was too small to believe that God cared enough about her transportation situation to church or any place she wanted to travel.

By thinking small and believing small you are rejecting the truth of God's Word. John 8:32, "*You shall know the truth, and the truth shall <u>make</u>* {build, create, construct, compose} *you free*." I often hear people quote it as "set" you free however, I can set my coffee cup down and it will remain in that exact position until I move it. Yet the word "make" indicates building, creating, constructing, and composing. All these words describe something is happening. When I know the truth of God through the Holy Spirit something begins to happen inside of me outside of me and through me.

Bondage isn't always in the 'world'…bondage is often more devastating in the church since we refuse to acknowledge it, so we learn to live with it. The church has many dark secrets that we don't talk about. This causes unresolved issues to fester thus we produce wounded Christians with wounded spirits that produce bitterness rather than vision.

Inspiring change was produce in the hearts of millions as a man from Georgia penned one of the most famous speeches of all time entitled, "I have a dream." In a time of racial darkness throughout America Martin Luther King Jr. followed his heart and conveyed his vision to the people. His vision became a reality but at a cost.

Your vision is going to cost you; it may be your resources, your time, your commitment, and your reputation. Individuals of vision are often criticized and miss understood because their actions are looked upon as pride and arrogance...trying to be better than others. As long as you remain in the same trap of disparity, poverty, and just get by; no one will challenge you. It is only after realizing your potential in Christ that conflict begins. This type of reaction may be because Godly vision exposes the shortcomings in others who tried and failed because they did not follow the blueprint presented by the Holy Spirit.

> Exodus 13:3, Moses, said unto the people, "Remember this
> day (mark this day), in which you came out from Egypt,
> out of the <u>house of bondage</u> (the place of your slavery).
> For the Lord has brought you out by his mighty power.

God is a God on the move...to the children of Israel He was a cloud by day and pillar of fire by night (Exodus 13:21). Most times when God moves you from one place to another it requires leaving behind things you consider important. Most of us carry 'old luggage' that serves no purpose other than to hold us back or keep us down. So why do we continue to lug it from place to place?

You can't change where you have been, but you can change where you're going. Too often Christian's build their relationship to Jesus around the trials they have gone through. Their testimony becomes that of what they have gone through rather than how BLESSED they could be living. I heard a pastor while back talk of all the things he didn't do and as he went through his 'moral list' of pride you could cut the cloud of condemnation in the crowd. You could abstain from every event and gathering the world has to offer hid away in your home pretending to be holier then thou and miss completely the will of God. Jesus said feed my sheep, don't beat my sheep.

God never called us to hid within our four walls and point our finger at our neighbor and declare how righteous we are. Jesus went into the streets, the highways and by ways proclaiming the Father's love, mercy, and grace. Most people's impression of a Christian is the one you leave them. Remember the saying, "WWJD…What Would Jesus Do?"

Their badge of honor is the defeats they have endured. Some people NEVER experience the fullness of God because all their prayers consist of is asking God to meet their needs…what about your desires? Psalm 37:4, "*Delight yourself also in the Lord, And He shall give you the desires {request} of your heart.*" God wants to turn your unpleasant situation around today and beginning experiencing His blessing as a Believer…how could you bless other if you're not blessed? Don't become that sad Christian trying to save happy sinners.

Consider this; a person on a fixed income can't plan beyond their means since the monthly amount is already allocated for a specific purpose. For instance if they wanted to travel for vacation or purchase a new vehicle if their means doesn't provide for those luxuries then the only other alternative is to borrow but how can you borrow when you have no collateral?

That family or individual became a <u>captive of their limitation of their vision</u> and the best that they can do is hope that tomorrow will be different. The problem isn't the supply of money it's the vision that is in your heart. How do you see yourself? What you put in your heart will determine your outcome as long you are unwilling to change your circumstances…if you change your vision, you will change your circumstances.

Out of the abundance of the heart, the mouth speaks; in other words what is in your heart the mouth brings forth. It is manifested outwardly. I can choose to be healthily over sickness, prosperity over poverty, opportunity over problems, blessing over cursing the choice is mine. The definition of the word <u>blessed</u> is "To fill with benefits."

> Psalms 103:1-3, "Bless the LORD, O my soul;
> And all that is within me, *bless* His holy name!
> ² Bless the LORD, O my soul,
> **and forget not all His benefits:**
> ³ Who forgives all your iniquities (sins),
> Who heals all your diseases."
> Psalms 63:19, "Blessed *be* the Lord,
> *Who* <u>daily</u> loads us *with benefits,*
> The God of our salvation! Selah"

As a Native American or Blackfeet (Pikuni), I have a variety of excuses I could use to hold me down. I have every right to blame others for any difficulties in life if I so desire and most people would agree and feel sorry for me considering:

1. I was born on an poverty stricken Indian reservation
2. The government took everything I owned
3. Education wasn't deemed important in our family
4. Alcohol, drugs, and lack are common place in "Indian Country"
5. They say Christianity is a white man's religion, if that's the case a pick-up truck is a white man's invention and you see them on every Indian reservation...the list just goes on, and on, and on.

I choose to live a life that reflects Christ in my life. I do live on the Blackfeet Indian reservation because it is my home. It is where in have grown in the Lord and have witnessed a transformation spiritually, physically, and financially in my life because of the Word of God according to Romans 12:2, "*And be not <u>conformed to this world</u> but be ye <u>transformed by the renewing of your mind</u>, that ye may prove what is that good, and acceptable, and <u>perfect, will of God</u>.*" Since Jesus came into my life I have purpose, direction...I now have a vision for my life, for my family, and for my ministry.

Fulfillment of vision doesn't occur over night. Consider Joseph who was seventeen years old when he had his first vision (Genesis 37:2). It wasn't until thirteen years later at the age of thirty did he stand before Pharaoh (Genesis 41:46) and another nine years since the famine was in its second year that Joseph is (39) thirty-nine years old when his brothers bowed down before him and he reveals to them that he is their brother (Genesis 45:6) this was a total of twenty-two years he waited for the fulfillment of the vision to come to pass.

There is a song we sing in 'Indian Country" and the words go something like this, "I woke up early this morning and Jesus told me to hold on..." Sometimes holding on is the toughest thing to do when we live in a right now world. My experience with holding on has produced patience, trust, and peace in the midst of the storm as one songwriter said, "He may not come when you want Him, but He's right on time."

CHAPTER FIVE

She Called Me Sir

"Seasons & Cycles of our Lives"

As a child we would often congregate with our relatives formulating our own mini tribe since we were large in mass. Each family represent between ten to fifteen members and when you consider five to six families the numbers add up. The boys would ride bareback horses wildly, racing along the railroad track as visitors from America's east encountered their first "Real Indians" within the security of the Great Northern passenger train that was traveling west toward Glacier National Park.

All their 'white' faces would be glued to the window as our imaginary war party gently faded into the birch trees that covered the hillside. We often wondered where those countless pictures ended up or how the story was retold of these "Wild Montana Indians" who were attacking the train. What they didn't realize most of us boys were younger than twelve years old...we just looked mean and tough.

Just like boys everywhere we liked to tease, play tricks and laugh at others. However, there were times that the tables were turned on us and we became the joke. On the west part of Browning there is a museum that portrays the history of the Blackfeet and by the busload tourist would stop and study us from afar off. During one of these visitations we were once again on horseback about ten of us in the group.

Voices from across the road summon us asking if they could take pictures of us on our horses. We posed as if we were from some professional agency turning our horses this way and that way until the tourist begin to reload the bus. It was then a gentleman thanked us and offered us some money, which my older cousin accepted graciously. To our frustration he had given us "twenty-five" cents...one quarter to divide between ten hungry, thirsty boys.

Now I'm not a mathematician but I think that comes out to be two and a half cents a piece, even in those days two cents didn't go far, we just road off laughing at the ignorance of that white man who gave us Indian boys a quarter. He must have thought we had never seen money before. Well Manhattan was acquired for twenty-four dollars.

I consider myself blessed for having such a rich childhood filled with adventure and excitement. We were one of the few families that had the opportunity to leave the reservation for a season, traveling to places like Washington, California, and Oregon. These places filled my heart with desire to explore this great land of ours later as an adult.

Sometime back I was about to order at a fast food joint when the cashier asked, "How may I help you sir." I actually didn't reply until it dawned on me she was talking to me. When did I become a "Sir?" Isn't that the next step to a senior citizen? In our Blackfeet culture that would imply I'm nearing elder hood. As I sit here writing my youngest grandson who is less than a year old is resting on my knee playing with his first two teeth wow, how time has gone by since my train chasing days.

Everything Has Its Time

To everything *there is* a season,
A time for every purpose under heaven:
A time to be born,
And a time to die;
A time to plant,
And a time to pluck *what is* planted;
A time to kill,
And a time to heal;
A time to break down,
And a time to build up;
A time to weep,
And a time to laugh;
A time to mourn,
And a time to dance… (Ecclesiastes 3:1-4 NKJV)

If I were to write everything about my life it would fill volumes of books now whether you would read it or not is another story. Each time I'm called sir I want to reply with the proverbial joke, "You must mean my father…my name is Bill." While having my haircut in Great Falls, Montana the stylist spattered small talk one question after another about things that really didn't matter. One of her questions involved if I had any children and with eyes half closed I answered that I have five children and before she could respond I said, "As a matter of fact I have eight grand-children and counting."

She stepped backward in disbelief saying over and over again, "You're not old enough to have grandchildren" all the well looking to see if I would say, I'm just joking. As a matter of fact I do have grandchildren but I'm not the grandparent of my grandfather or grandmother. When they were in their early forties they looked old, they dressed old, and they even acted old.

Today we live in a world of youth appearance, I would like to think the Holy Spirit is keeping me young looking even though my years of sinning took some toll on me. There isn't anything wrong with wanting to remain young but no matter how you try and hold on to your youth something is eventually going to give. A little nip here a little tug there maybe some wrinkle cream, body gel, and that miracle of science hair dye…as they say whatever makes your day.

Our life is symbolic of seasons; first there is spring, which is the time of birth and new beginnings followed by summer a time of discoveries, adventure, and countless possibilities. The only problem with summer is we never want it to end, just like a young adult who wants to live life to its fullest occupying every moment of time. Then there is fall season when nature slows down reminding us of our many responsibilities and that life isn't about endless summers. Suddenly winter is upon us releasing the reality and chill of life…if we aren't sheltered during winter the elements will over take us.

The Blackfeet
"Pikuni"

I can't speak of my Christian life without relating who I'm as a Blackfeet man. Many Native American cultures including the Blackfeet (Pikuni) subscribe to the circle concept of life or better known as the "Medicine Wheel." The non-Native mind views life on a horizontal plane consisting of a beginning, middle section, and an end. This is a very restricted thought if it is a representation of life. You're born, you grow, and then you die. While within the Medicine Wheel or the circle there is no end. Life is a continuous especially after death. The Jewish people prescribe to this similar belief of seasons and the circle of life.

Within the Blackfeet culture our people of old; those before the European contact were men of prayer and fasting. Among the tribal leaders rested the strength of the tribe since they were men of vision who protected the integrity of the people. They were men who gave of themselves tirelessly whether it was food, horses, or spiritual guidance. Their lives were examples to the people in a time of approaching transition.

Change was evident just as the sun would rise each morning in the east and usher in the darkness to the west; change was coming among the Blackfeet. One of the greatest leaders of the Blackfoot Confederacy that numbered 40,000 – 50,000 was Chief White

Calf. It is said he was a man of great conviction who prayed daily for the well being of his people. He wasn't a violent man but if forced into a corner he would fight for what was right even if that meant leaving his home and going to Washington, D.C. to lobby on behalf of his people during the late 1800's and into the new century.

As the traditional lands of the Blackfeet begin to shrink because of government treaties, Executive Orders, and outright thievery White Calf press the United States government to consider future generations of Blackfeet (Pikuni) and stop the eradication of our land that once went as far north to Edmonton, Alberta Canada, south to the Yellowstone River near present day Billings, Montana, then to the eastern boarder of what is now the North Dakota, Montana state line, then westward to the natural fortress of the Great Rocky Mountains.

Chief White Calf convinced the Blackfoot (Siksika) Nation to alter their ways and to adopt what the white man was offering because he wanted to see his people survive, rather than die. He realized the days of buffalo gathering was gone, the days of roaming the prairie was over, the Blackfeet were being confined to a reservation...a way of life they had never known. Chief White Calf knew within his heart there was no going back. He died at the age of 80 in 1903 alone in Washington, D.C. speaking on behalf of the Blackfeet who had no voice.

Our reservation today is 1.5 million acres which is about the same size as Glacier National Park however, about 1/3 of the reservation is owned by non-tribal members and our remaining land mass continues to be taken by outsiders. So really the battles that Chief White Calf fought have never ended only the times. Many Blackfeet tribal members believe we are strangers in our own land considering the negative actions of land owning non-members who post their land with "No Hunting and No Trespassing" signs and patrol the land as past U.S. Calvary soldiers waiting for an Indian attack.

I speak of White Calf because he embodies a fundamental element of my life, you'll understand that in a moment. My father is Grayson Old Chief, and his father was John Old Chief also named "Shoots First," his father was Old Chief "Ah-Gan-Na" (This is the Blackfeet name I now have which was given to me by George & Molly Kicking Woman in 1999). Old Chief's father was Big Painted Lodge (not much is known of him), and his father was <u>Chief White Calf</u>.

My grand father's Old Chief (Ah-Gan-Na) and John Old Chief were some of the last traditional spiritual leaders among the Blackfeet along with their wife's. They were there in the time of history when that way of life was common. They didn't learn it from a book, they wrote the book. Leadership isn't about an elected position, leadership is within the heart. It is a gift from the people, if no one is following then you're not a leader.

My father choose to accept the Gospel message and rejected the traditional 'Medicine Pipe, Beaver Bundle, and the Medicine Lodge' or Sun Dance of his father. This wasn't an easy decision considering we had lived this way for centuries. In retrospect my grandfather's believed that their way was a gift from the Creator

(A-Pist-Too-Doo-Ke)…it was what had kept them spiritually strong during those challenging years of change. Their songs, prayers, and dances reflected reverence for the Creator who had entrusted them as stewards over this precious land called Blackfeet Country.

At the gravesite of my father my first cousin Paul "Windy" Old Chief approached me and ask if he could sing our family song for my dad (society song). I was surprise that we even had a traditional family song in the Blackfeet language. After saying yes, Paul sang the most beautiful song I ever heard. Now picture this Rocky Mountains is the backdrop, hundreds of people are gathered, Paul and three other gentlemen are holding buckskin hand drums. Paul's words follow first then the others join in repeating in harmony. Tears begin to flow and I never was as proud as I was that moment of our people. Just think this song has been song for countless years before my father or me. This is when I decided I had to find out who I was as a Blackfeet man even though I was a Christian.

As I look back on my family tree they were leaders among our people my grandfather John also served as our tribal police chief at one time, my father was a Pastor and spiritual leader among our people. One day I was elected to our tribal council and served as the Blackfeet Tribal Chairman and while in that position sitting in my office I would wonder, "How did I arrive here?" Sounds like a simple question but it took years before it was answered. It was only after discovering my connection to Chief White Calf did I realize that God had directed my path. Once again I have been blessed and honored by the Blackfeet people to serve on the tribal council.

The steps of a good man are ordered by the Lord… (Psalm 37:23)." I thought about Moses who was born a slave, delivered into the water and was rescued as a prince of Egypt. Who would have thought that an enemy of Egypt would one day lead the children of Israel to freedom. David said, "Thou prepares a table before me in the presence of mine enemies: thou anointed my head with oil; my cup runneth over (Psalm 23:5)."

You may be in the land of your enemies, but if *God be for you who can be against you?* A thousand shall fall at thy side, and ten thousand at thy right hand; but it shall not come nigh thee. But he was wounded for our transgressions, he was bruised for our iniquities: the chastisement of our peace was upon him; and with his stripes we are healed. Now that's something to praise God for…by his stripes we are healed. Jesus healed my past he healed my mind, he healed my heart.

I don't have to live under the bondage of past government failures, I don't have to be a spiritual slave to the hardships of Egypt (this world or this reservation) as the old songwriter said, "He set me free, He set me. Glory to God He set me free!" I refuse to blame others for a past I have no domination over. I will not give anyone that kind of power over my life or the lives of my family…"Thou shalt be <u>blessed</u> above all people (Deuteronomy 7:14)." Bless the Lord. O my soul, and forget not all his benefits: Who forgives all thine iniquities; who healeth all thy diseases (Psalm 103:2-3)."

I strongly believe that when Jesus died on the cross of Calvary he said 'it was finished' there isn't anything I can add to make the plan of salvation more complete…it is finished! Jesus came to do away with a law that man could not live according too. The law became a bondage to mankind and man begins to fail the moment it was presented to him. I'm no longer a slave to the bondage of sin; I'm no longer a slave to the bondage of my past. I don't serve creation I serve the Creator of all, Lord of lord's and the King of kings. I have discovered there are benefits to serving Jesus and it's not just in the sweet by and by. The bondage of alcohol that plagued our family was broken in my father's life, it was destroyed in my life and I pass on that promise to my children and grandchildren.

I bless my children everyday through prayer. I bless my grandchildren in the same manner…speaking blessing into their spirit again and again. According to Galatians 3, if we belong to Christ, then we are Abraham's seed and heirs according to the promise. As heirs we inherit the "Blessing of Abraham" which is spiritually, physically, and financially." This is the promise I proclaim over my family on a daily basis.

Galatians 3:13-14 (New International Version)
Christ redeemed us from the curse of the law by becoming a curse for us, for it is written: "Cursed is everyone who is hung on a tree." He redeemed us in order that the blessing given to Abraham might come to the Gentiles through Christ Jesus, so that by faith we might receive the promise of the Spirit.

Galatians 4:5-7 (New International Version)
To redeem those under law, that we might <u>receive the full rights of sons</u>. Because you are sons, God sent the Spirit of his Son into our hearts, the Spirit who calls out, "Abba, Father." So <u>you are no longer a slave</u>, but a son; and since you are a son, God has made you also an heir.

This is the reason I awake each morning, look westward to the Rocky Mountains even before I wash my face and thank God for all he has done in my life. I once was blind but now I see I was lost but now I'm found. "I am crucified with Christ: nevertheless I live; yet not I, but Christ liveth in me: and the life which I now live in the flesh <u>I live by the</u> <u>faith of the Son of God, who loved me, and gave himself for me</u>." (Galatians 2:20)

Recently I had the privilege of visiting with a Jewish Rabbi at my home I felt so honored and blessed to have him in my home. Before he left he prayed a blessing over my home and family but while we were visiting I asked him this question just for verification. You know sometimes we just need to hear it from the horse's mouth so to speak. I asked him concerning the 'covenant promises' that were given to Abraham, Isaac, and Jacob (Israel) concerning their importance to the Jewish people. He replied that the Jewish still hold to those promises. Then I asked him what about us (Gentiles / non-Jewish people) as we accept Christ do we truly become heirs and joint heirs to those same promises? Yes, yes, and yes was his reply.

That's all I needed to hear. Now I believe even more strongly that God wants to release goodness into my life. That day I took spiritual keys and proclaimed I was going to use them with authority. If my Jewish brother is blessed and we have the same Father...then I'm blessed, blessed, blessed. You're blessed also. I learned a new saying; "There is nothing wrong with God. There is nothing wrong with the Word. There is nothing wrong with you!" we are blessed.

The very first summer that I was "saved" we were at a camp meeting near the rocky mountain front along the Cut Bank Creek. Without thinking I begin to speak out loud concerning the beauty of the mountains, the sky, and about the creation of God. "Man these mountains are beautiful, just look how awesome they are they seem to go on forever."

Unaware of the white haired lady next to from Lapwai, Idaho she asked, "Where are you from son?" I said from here. You talk as if this is the first time you have seen these mountains? My reply was, "It is." It was the first time I had seen them with the clarity of the Holy Spirit. Sure I had driven past them summer after summer but now I had a clean heart and a clean mind before they were just a place to go and party. What a change the Lord makes in our lives even the countryside looked different.

Isn't it amazing how God cleans our lives? How he takes want was dirty and good for nothing (sin nature) and in a moment just because we ask, accept, and believe a total transformation is manifested before our eyes...the world can't understand this but it happens because of the blood of Jesus and His love for us.

Muriel (Shining Sea or Myrrh)

The two biggest influences in my life are my wife and Jesus. What she couldn't change Jesus did. From the moment I noticed her I knew I wanted her in my life and the best part about the whole thing was she lived just across the street form me. It took a few years before we actually became serious with each other and to my surprise she admitted she told he mother, "See that guy over there? One day I'm going to marry him." Now that's what I call VISION…a mighty woman of valor (Blackfeet women are like the Canadian Mounties…they always get their man).

When we eventually did marry I consider myself to be a Christian even though I was living for the devil and she was Catholic at heart. We never augured over religion except when it came time to baptize our first daughter Karrilyn, she wanted to baptize her in the Catholic Church and I fought it tooth and nail. I threaten her that if she did not to come home…I was going to stay mad. She did it anyway, she came home, and we continued to live our lives without Christ. For that one brief moment I was willing to fight for my "church." As the scripture says, "Train up a child in the way he should go and when he is old he will not depart from it." (Proverbs 22:6)

In the early spring of 1980, May 21st to be exact I went to an old Pentecostal church where there were less than nine people on a Wednesday night and I asked Jesus into my life. The minister didn't even make an alter call the conviction of the Holy Ghost was so strong upon me I literally ran before him and begin to ask God to forgive me. Two nights later on a Friday night service in the same church the Spirit of God came upon me while the congregation was singing, I raised my hands toward heaven I was instantly filled with the Holy Spirit and begin to speak a heavenly language.

From that moment on our lives have never been the same. Ecclesiastes 4:9-10, "Two are better than one; because they have a good report for their labor. For if they fall, the one will lift up his follow..." This scripture has never been truer than in our lives. We have endured the storms of life, huddled in the valley of bewilderment, and have see the mountaintop only because we have had each other.

Today people are so easily moved and unwilling to fight for what they love or once loved. The moment trouble arises within their marriage it is off to conquer another life only to realize they have captured the same metaphorical beast. They may have a different face, a different body, but the same issues begin to control the situation and the whirlwind of frustration, anger, jealously, and bitterness becomes evident once again.

"Who can find a <u>virtuous</u> (righteous - honorable - good) woman? For her price is far above rubies." I often perform two - three weddings per year and there is a statement within the wedding vow that says, "Marriage is a <u>divine</u> (Godly) institution, and we are taught in the Scripture that it is to be honored among all men." Another part that both parties repeat is, "...will you love her/ him, honor her/him, comfort her, and cherish her, in health and in sickness, in prosperity and in adversity; and forsake all others remain true to her as long as you both live?

If I were to describe Muriel it would be similar to this found in: Proverbs 31:11-28 (NCV)

[11] Her husband trusts her completely.
With her, he has everything he needs.
[12] She does him good and not harm
for as long as she lives.
[13] She looks for wool and flax
and likes to work with her hands.
[14] She is like a trader's ship,
bringing food from far away.
[17] She does her work with energy,
and her arms are strong.
[18] She knows that what she makes is good.
Her lamp burns late into the night.
[20] She welcomes the poor
and helps the needy.
[21] She does not worry about her family when it snows,
for all her household are clothed with scarlet.

[23] Her husband is known in the gates, when
he sitteth among the elders of the land.
[25] Strength and honor are her clothing.
She looks forward to the future with joy.

[26] She openeth her mouth with wisdom:
And in her tongue is the law of kindness.
[27] She watches over her family
and never wastes her time.
[28] Her children rise up, and
Call her blessed; her husband also…

Often we visit during the evening after a long day or during a ride to a distant city our conversations often are those of family, our walk with God, or the things we have been through. We have been together for so long and through so much that people often forget that Muriel had a maiden name. One day someone asked her about her brother saying, "I forgot you used to be a Lahr...I just thought you were always an Old Chief."

I'm proud and blessed that she has "always been an Old Chief" my Old Chief. Most women would never have put up with what she had to with me. The first house we lived in was a one-bedroom trailer and no running water, which is really tough living in a northern Montana winter. She would shower at her parent's house and I would shower at my parents. Other than that I would have to carry water for the toilet (bathroom). Most times we were without a vehicle so we walked, held hands and continue to love each other in the poverty of our youth. Today that has changed considerably since she now carries the water.

Most of our dinners during Thanksgiving and Christmas comprised of dinning with either Muriel's family or mine in the past however, lately we have begun to gather at our home with our children and grandchildren that is located in the Cut Bank Creek bottom, sheltered by cotton wood trees and acres of room for children to run and play. We moved into the country more than seventeen years ago and discovered it suited us just fine.

Blackfeet people are sometimes superstitious concerning ghost, shadows, and yes Bigfoot and children will often ask my grandchildren, "Aren't you guys afraid to live in the country, do ghost ever bother you?" Adults have even asked me that and I just tell them the only ghost I'm concerned with is the Holy Ghost. Some of these are church people, my, my. "A fools mouth is his destruction, and his lips are the snare of his soul" (Proverbs 18:7).

It's amazing that just a shot time back there was just Muriel and I, now our grown children have started their own families and through it all Muriel has been there for every one of them. Sometimes I'll hear the grandchildren calling her 'mom' then quickly correct themselves. If she was telling this story the details would be more complete because her mind is able to recapture times, dates, and names as if just happened whereas with me I have to dig deep into the vault of my mind and frequently look at notes.

In the early days as change became more apparent in my life, Muriel really didn't understand how God was transforming me but she welcomed it, remember she wasn't raised in a Christian home and much of what she was witnessing was very foreign to her. Soon after I committed my life to Jesus she asked Jesus into her heart.

I have watched her grow from a young girl into a woman of wisdom, strength, and courage. She has prayed morning, noon, and night for the safe return of both our daughter Kash who was in Iraq twice and our son Shawn who severed two tours in Iraq and one tour in Afghanistan as a U.S. Marine sergeant.

She was there for our grandsons when they had their tonsils removed and they cried with pain asking their 'grandmother to pray for them. She stayed late into the night and early into the morning with our daughters when they gave birth. My job is spoiling my grandchildren, which is a lot harder than going into a delivery room.

When she is at work people often approach her for prayer and she'll make time for them. There are times she returns from the IGA grocery store (**I**ndians **G**rab **A**nything) and she'll have a number of prayer requests that we bring before the Lord again and again. People have learned that they can call upon Muriel for prayer whether they are family, friend, and at times even foe.

God has truly blessed my life and I'm often the one recognized at events for whatever reason but always in the back of my mind I own any success in my life to Muriel. The saying is true, "For every successful man there is a great woman beside him." By the way we just celebrated our 39th wedding anniversary November 9th.

Lately I have watched elder couples walking together holding hands apparently in love and quietly in my heart I ask God to let me grow old with Muriel… "Let us be the couple walking in love with each other just as the day we met." God truly has blessed me with my soul mate. A woman who is loved by many.

CHAPTER SIX

My Fathers Blessing

"That the blessing of Abraham
Might come on the Gentiles through Jesus Christ"
Galatians 3:14

Before I really understood anything about "The Fathers Blessing or Covenant" within the Word of God I received a blessing from my father. Just before my dad went home to be with Jesus he asked if his children would gather at his house. One by one we stood before him as he proceed to pray over us as individuals and pronounce a blessing into our lives. This was different than just a prayer meeting he was instilling destiny, vision, and purpose into his adult children. My father had a ninth-grade education yet, excelled in every area of his life as he allowed the Holy Spirit to fashion him into the very scriptures that he devoured each day of his life as a man who loved Jesus.

Sometime later I begin to hear ministers preach about the "Fathers Blessing" and the need for that specific word within the church since so many men young and old alike were displace by not hearing their father speak blessing into their life.

Like other fathers of his time there wasn't much emotion or open affection emulating from him toward his children…may be with the daughters however, with the boys we were required to act like boys and that meant, "Boys don't cry." You were required to grow strong and be able to defend yourself. To be honest I can't recall one time as a child that my dad openly hugged us and said I love you. Now this didn't leave any emotional scares or cause me to become dysfunctional and start robbing banks or stealing candy from children. I just thought it was normal for boys to be boys.

As he became a grandfather his true emotions flourished as he would tenderly hold his grandsons and kiss them gently over their entire face all the while speaking only words the child was suppose to understand. I promised myself that when I had children it would be different and I have tried with all my heart to fulfill that within my sons and daughters. At any given opportunity I pray over my children and grandchildren proclaiming the "Blessing of Abraham" in their life concerning the spiritual, physical, and financial blessing that God has provided for them as heirs in the kingdom of God.

For a while I wrestled with the same insecurities that my own father must have encountered yet, I continued to break that invisible barrier that was trying to separate me form my sons. I guess at times it is just easier for the mother to care for the children then for the father to be a father. Impatience, harshness, and unwilling to listen are a fathers worst enemies when he is trying to connect with his children. A child will only open up when they feel safe and if a father is always short or harsh with the children they will eventually drift from that type of treatment.

When you are raised in an environment without open affection you soon learn to identify it in other ways such as hunting trips, playing softball with the adults, or even working side by side with your father. I do remember my dad teaching me how to drive when I was seven or eight years old. After that anything that had an engine I would drive including an old Ford tractor. I remember him buying me little cowboy clothes then buying me my first car when I was sixteen years and then another car the following year. To me that type of love spoke louder than words. Oh yes, he was proud of me when I enlisted into the United States Army because he told me so. As a matter of fact he was the one who wrote me letters while I was in "boot camp" and not my mother as most would think.

Life went on but it wasn't until I surrendered my life to Christ that our relationship truly became father/son. During my first years of being a Christian I traveled with my parents and helped them at their meetings on the Crow Indian reservation and in Alberta Canada on the Indian reserves which we called, "Across the line." My father was an anointed Prophet and song leader. He spent many hours in prayer travailing before the throne of God to move in his life. His services were always filled with excitement and powerful releases of the Holy Spirit.

I would tell Muriel that my dad was the best preacher I ever heard and I meant it. I would get excited to hear him minister since one of his sayings was, "I want fresh bread from the bakeries of Heaven." He was a man who believed in receiving a fresh word from God according to the "Lord's Prayer" in Luke 11:3. The song that is best remembered by many is, "Up above my head, I hear music in the air."

"A Man of God"

When I recall my father I envision a man lost in the Bible and especially the Old Testament, he wasn't a scholar from any Bible college yet; his ability to understand and pronounce biblical names was remarkable...he put most Bible educated men to shame. During my rebellious years as a teen I would wonder into the house well after midnight and could hear my dad crying out to God what seemed like hours. He wasn't bashful about his petitions that he brought before the Lord either. He could pray just as well in our Blackfeet language as in English since Blackfeet was his first language.

Like father, like son I soon begin to follow in his footsteps as a minister of the Gospel and with this promotion I found myself often learning from my dad concerning the revelations of God's Word. We would sit for hours as ministers these are the moments I begin to receive "My father's blessing." As my Pastor he would ask me to do the praise and worship and every once in a while he would ask me to preach now that's what I call a father's blessing. I felt so honored he would want to listen to me minister the Word.

His convictions have gone unmatched in the world we live in today. I remember him preaching about the sin of adultery (Mark 10:11) and that it wasn't welcome in the church and especially with ministers of the Gospel. Yes he offended some but he held true to his convictions right to the very end. He believed in the

power of the cross of Christ Jesus and that God was a holy God…
he was uncompromising but always fair.

One of the most profound statements my dad ever made was of a
vision another person had that he was sharing with the church. In
the vision a man was in hell and a mass of people were scattered
throughout the area all laying facedown. There was an individual
who would grab the hair of a person and pull them up to expose
their face. This he did again and again stepping over the countless
bodies. The man receiving the vision asked God, "What is he
looking for? He is looking for the preacher that lied to him…
since he ended up in hell the preacher that lied to him must be
there also."

I never heard him apologize for what he preached as a matter of
fact he said, "If I have offended you by something I have said while
preaching I will apologize to you personally, if the Word of God
has offended you then you have to take that up with God." His
compassion for the lost was exemplified by his commitment to lay
down his life in the service of the Gospel. My father gave all he
had into serving the Lord as he ministered throughout Canada and
the southwestern United States in America's unforgotten Indian
reservations. He had the privilege of leading many to Christ and
according to the scripture, "He that winneth souls is wise."

I was frequently thrilled about his return from some distance land
and ready to debrief him concerning the wonders to behold and
the miracles to be told. Stories of salvation by the multitude, both
young and old. Healings that were descriptions right from the
pages of the New Testament…the blind see, the lame walking,

and unclean spirits coming out of those who had been in bondage for countless years.

My father was like the traditional Blackfeet warrior returning from some distance country with the spoils of war only his were the victories that God had given because of his obedience, devotion, and love for the people. Recently a Pastor friend of ours shared with his church how my father influenced his ministry. He said, "Grayson Old Chief was a true Prophet. Many people call themselves prophets but Grayson was a Prophet."

He went on to describe how my dad showed up at his house one summer afternoon after driving more than ten hours asking for a drink of water and then sharing with him what God was about to do in his life. After he drank his water he got back into his car and drove back home. Wow! That occurred more than thirty-years ago and that church continues to grow as of today. In a recent meeting with that specific Pastor he announced they were going to break ground on a larger church for that community. Today that church is standing strong as a symbol of hope and light on the southern edge of the Crow reservation. His last remake was, your dad's word are still coming to pass today!

Now think about that. He didn't ask for a church meeting or a place to spend the night in the best hotel...he didn't ask for an offering. He just spoke the word as directed by the Holy Ghost. That's a picture right out of the Old Testament. From those words spoken that man became a committed Christian and fulltime Pastor on the Crow Indian Reservation helping change the lives of his people with the good news of Christ Jesus.

My father was a man who had seen many visions of people and events. God would show his individuals in a specific meeting long before the service begin and what God was going to do for them. As the service proceeded my dad would recognize them from the vision and by faith call them forth and proclaim what God had shown him just hours before. Just as in the vision he would pray over their need and witness the power of God do the rest. This became commonplace, which caused most buildings to be filled to capacity time and time again.

One time he and my mother were having dinner with a mayor in a small Montana town and a picture on the wall caught his attention. He asked the mayor, "Where is this place?" which the mayor replied "Ship Rock, New Mexico." He later told my mother this is where we are going to be preaching…this is the place God showed my in a vision. It wasn't long after that they were being ushered from one community to the next on the Navajo Indian reservation preaching with signs and wonders following the Word of God. This continued well over a month and then many return trips to fulfill the calling of God.

My dad would often say, "Bill, your gift will make room for you." You will never have to promote yourself. This phrase has become true in my life and whenever it happens I am reminded of his divine wisdom.

My dad also had another side to him which attracted people to him and that was his ability to share stories and basically be humorous. One story I remember that was told about him came from my uncle of a time before they knew Jesus. There was a group of them in their younger days that were drinking or as the younger people would say today, "partying." Before long they ran out of money and options to gain money so my dad suggested they remove one of the solid wooden doors from the hinges and sell it…that they did. My uncle remarked there were strange comments from those in the community who had seen them carrying the door around town since they had no car to haul it.

Another time my dad related the story of my first cousin who was telling a story of his "cowboy days" now if you knew this person you would know he isn't the cowboy type. I don't think I have ever seen him in a pair western boots to be truthful. Anyway my cousin was really into his story of riding this bucking horse. He would describe how the horse turned this way and that, of how he just about lost it before the eight second count. This is when my dad interrupted my cousin's story by commenting, "And then you had to put another quarter into the machine." Those listening to the story all begin to laugh un-controllable as my cousin became very up set. In the long run even my cousin saw the humor it what had just happened. You just couldn't stay mad at my dad.

On one occasion as he was preaching he told the story of a poor old man from a small Indian community in Montana. He described the man as being frail, bent over, and short in statue. He was often in worn out and soiled clothing, which added to his age. This old man entered a country cafe one winter evening and after looking over the menu asked the waitress how much is the coffee and she replied seventy-five cents a cup and <u>refills are free</u>. Quick to respond the old man said, "I'll have the refill please."

Accounts like this helped shape my values and perceptions concerning my Christian walk. If my dad could laugh and make others laugh I realized it was all right to be happy and not pious to prove my love for Jesus.

Some people think they have to be 'pious' all the time in order to appear holy to others. So they don't laugh. They don't smile. They just stare at you mean looking and they wonder why no one is getting saved in their ministry. Maybe it's because they have the "Ministry of Meanness" rather than meekness. I heard a man once say, "We have too many sad Christians trying to save happy sinners." This is true! Proverbs 11:30b declares, "…He that winneth souls is wise."

Those who knew my father respected him as the "Man of God" and one person who esteemed my dad above all was my first cousin Ella Faye who lived in Washington State. It was her practice to invite my dad to her house whenever he was in her locality. Most times it was either for breakfast or dinner.

One morning as he sat down to breakfast with her he said to her in a troubling voice, "Ella, I had a dream about you last night." To her surprise she stopped eating and gave complete attention to what was about to be said. The entire house took on an eerie silence. What secret had God revealed to him about her?

In the dream the Rapture of the Church had taken place he told her and all around me people were going up however I wasn't moving. He describe the panic and fear that filled the atmosphere of those who were not leaving and at that moment he told her you begin to lift upward and without thinking he said I grabbed a hold of your back soon we were both nearing haven. As they approached the "Pearly Gates" St. Peter greeted them saying, "Grayson it's so good to see you we have been waiting for you, come on in… but you will have to leave you donkey outside."

It took my cousin a few moment to realize he had been teasing with her, slowly a smile formed on her face and said, "Honest uncle you're bad." Eventually every one at the table was laughing. Later she confessed how terrified she was when he said, I had a dream about you."

Throughout my travels in the ministry I have run across individuals who have know my dad and each one describes how they miss him and how he was a blessing to their life. Recently I was ministering at one of his old friends in Washington State. This pastor continued to tell me how my dad influenced his life and ministry…I just listened with delight considering how blessed I was for a father who shared Christ with me and never let me go, who would pray late into the night and early morning saying, "Jesus save my children, save Bill."

The years have pass since he has gone but to be honest with you there are times I hear his voice deep in my spirit as he speaks to me concerning my walk with the Lord. I believe this to be true since his words always came from the Word of God, which are the same yesterday, today, and forever. Once he came to me in a dream and spoke some powerful words that changed the direction of my life. The next morning I heeded those words and have never regretted his wisdom. He spoke to me when no other had the courage or insight as to what I was dealing with. All he said was, "Bill it's time to come home."

Just recently Muriel and I had supper with two couples in Yakima, Washington who shared passionately of how their lives were transformed by the words spoken into them by my father the Prophet and how that word spoken years ago is now coming to pass in their life. One of the gentlemen recommitted his life to serving Jesus and was delivered from alcohol and cigarettes has produced his first music CD and plans to do others in the near future. I'm blessed to have witnessed the fulfillment of God's word in their lives and it just gets better and better.

He once invited me to the Crow Indian reservation where he was to minister over the weekend beginning at a community called "Black Lodge"…that three days turned into 13 days, going from one church to the next. It is then I told him I'm going home. I have been washing my clothes over and over again. You said three days of ministering, not thirteen, I only brought three changes for church. So after service that night in Pryor, Montana (after being asked to hold another week-long revival) I headed north for Blackfeet Country and my dad following closely.

CHAPTER SEVEN

The Medicine of God

"A merry heart doeth good like a medicine:
But a broken spirit drieth the bones."
Proverbs 17:22

I heard a story recently about a young man who was sitting next to a single blond woman on the airplane and they were talking. Soon the man asked the young woman, "What kind of men do you like?" she said I just love Native American men because they are tall, handsome, with a permanent tan (sounds like Blackfeet men). Then I like Jewish men who are intellectual and successful. But my weakness is for southern men because of their manner of speech. She then asked the young man, "By the way what is your name?" He replied, "Geronimo Goldstein...but my friends call me Bubba."

Fourteen months after Muriel and I became Christians we decided to move about fifteen-miles northwest of Browning under the shadows of the Rocky Mountains. It was the kind of place any mountain man would have loved to raise his family. I would ride horseback nearly everyday and late into the evening. During this time we were allowed to hunt year around on the Blackfeet Indian Reservation, which was great. And I often brought home a deer.

Nowadays the tribe has us buying hunting license, confined to a short season with talk of implementing orange vest next...I should just start hunting off the reservation since I'd have a better chance at an elk. Well that's another story in itself, back to my country story. The hardest part of moving into the countryside was no television.

This was before the small satellite dishes of today that are so common. If you were willing to shell out $2,500 - $3,500 dollars you could get one of those huge dishes that TBN and other Christian networks use to beam signals around the world, only this was for your personal home use. Every time you wanted to change the signal you would have to go outside and hand-crank your dish.

Now I wasn't "TV bound" as some would say but I did enjoy watching Magnum P.I. which was my only weakness of the flesh to be honest. There was just something cool about a red sports car, a friend with his own chopper, and a life by the Hawaiian beach, sleeping in most of the day and no bills to pay...just your own private bungalow. So each week I would run to town at my parents and watch only that show.

After a while someone told me that they used to place an <u>old steel bed spring</u> on the hillside and point their house antenna at it to receive the local television stations. Now you have to put this in perspective since we only received three channels and one of them came from Lethbridge, Alberta Canada I was reaching out in desperation.

At this point I was willing to try anything since I couldn't afford the luxury of a "TBN" type satellite. During the late Fall when no one was watching me I gathered up a one hundred foot electrical cord, orange in color, about fifty feet of television cable that connects from the television to the antenna and placed my television set between the house and a barbwire fence that ran up the hill next to our home.

My thought was this, "If the fence goes to the top of the hill that would be better than dragging an old steel bedspring half a mile up the hill." With the TV in the field (on the ground) I ran the antenna wire to the fence and connected one piece to different wires so not to cross them (as if that mattered). I then connected the electrical orange wire to the plug in at the house and to my television. Holding my breath and on my stomach, turning my head every once in a while toward the road so no one would catch me…I turned on my television and to my amazement there was snow.

It wasn't snowing because of the late fall season; it was snow on my television every channel that I turned it to was snow, snow, and more snow. I think I even ask the Lord to let a channel come in. I fumbled with the set for about forty-five minutes or more wondering why it didn't work for me. I checked and rechecked the wire connections to no avail. I wasn't caught in this foolish act but I did have the feeling the same person who gave me the advice was watching me.

Looking back now I laugh at my desperation. That year without television was probably one of the best years of my life because I prayed and studied the Bible constantly. My nights were filled with prayer and my days with God's word. The distractions of the world coming into my living room were replaced by the solitude of the Spirit of God.

The hunger that I had to know more of Jesus begin to manifest in my life. It was as if the scriptures were coming alive before my very eyes. Often we would have visitors from town who would share a dinner or cook out with us and always our conversations would revert to the goodness of God.

"I saw the Light"

One late evening after church on a Friday night Muriel and I were asked by a young lady to pray with her because she wanted to receive the baptism of the Holy Ghost with the evidence of speaking in tongues. She invited us to her home where she lived with her elderly mother and young child.

After explaining to her the process and how "easy" I received the Holy Spirit I assured her to expect the same. I reminder her that it is a gift from God…all she had to was accept the gift. To my delight within minutes she was praying with tears streaming down her cheeks and I thought now this is easy however, this was short lived. She was like the little red train that almost reached the mountain peak only to slip back down the hill. The first time this happened wasn't that disappointing we just started up the hill again.

After an hour or so I became tired since it was well into the early morning and I begin to wonder if anything was going to be accomplished concerning her request. Like any good born-again Christian we shouted. We rebuked the devil. We even shook her lips hoping to help the Holy Ghost do His job. Now remember we were not much older then she was in the Lord. Zeal without wisdom can be dangerous. However I wasn't about to walk away from this challenge. Everyone in the room became quite out of exhaustion I stepped back from her to gather my thoughts and consider a different strategy. All the while she was quietly saying, "Jesus, Jesus, thank you Jesus" standing near the kitchen table with her eyes closed.

As I leaned up against the wall my back touched the light switch and for a few seconds the light above our head flashed off and on to our surprise there was a piercing scream that startled us all and without warning the young lady begin to speak in other tongues under the power of the Holy Ghost. No one was praying with her. No one was laying hands on her…the Holy Spirit just came upon her. This went on for another thirty or forty minutes. At one point her mother who was hard of hearing was waken by the commotion and entered the room where we were and said, "You guys will have to turn down that music, it's just too loud" then went back into her bedroom. All the while we just stood there quietly watching what was transpiring before us in bewilderment.

When the spiritual dust settled the young woman was so happy she just kept thanking us for praying with her, then she said these words, "I was just about to give up and was thinking maybe this isn't for me. All I could say was Jesus." She said then suddenly I saw a flash of light (remember her eyes were closed) and it was just like lighting shoot through my body and I begin to speak in tongues.

To this day I have never told her it was me leaning up against the light switch but as they say God works in mysterious ways. What she didn't realize we were all about ready to give up then came Jesus when all hope was gone. That young lady has matured into a spiritual powerhouse for the Lord. She is a woman of prayer and fasting and continues to touch the lives of others because she refused to give up.

"Laughter is good medicine"

Have you ever noticed a person that makes others laugh and feel good always has people around them? When I was in the "world" there was this individual we would pickup if just for a few hours just because he made us laugh. We knew he was the biggest liar in town but that's what made his stories funny. Right from go he would begin telling jokes, stories and act them out. We would laugh until tears filled our eyes or as my minister buddy Gabe once said, "I laughed so hard I had tears in my ears." Now that's funny in any language.

As a matter of fact most of the people I hung out with knew how to make me laugh or I would do the same for them. Maybe that's why we never wanted to go home we laughed at others and laughed at ourselves sometimes over the smallest matters. Now this is the heartbreaking portion of the story. After becoming a Christian I discovered it was considered a sin by some to be happy, to laugh, or just to enjoy life. Now that may be over stating it but that's what it seemed like because of the observation of others. I remember one winter into our second year as Christians a group of young people would gather at our home and we would play board games, drink coffee, and laugh well into the early morning.

One must take into consideration most of us came out of very difficult life styles where drugs and alcohol was a major factor. Now we had discovered we could enjoy life without destroying our physical bodies or committing spiritual suicide. Some of the older folks in the church got wind of what we were doing and became critical of our activities.

In their judgment this was ungodly and un-Christian like. It was almost as if they would have us doing what we did in the past then to be serving God as young happy Christians who were making an impact within our community and on the Blackfeet Indian reservation. Again I may have over stated the issue however they became very angry and demanded we stop.

Recently I heard a minister say once a week he would go to confession and was given a specific amount of prayers to pray. "I would confess to drinking, smoking, cussing, and chasing woman. Then I would go do it all over again." After becoming a Christian he continued to confess a few more times out of habit. He then confessed to attending a Pentecostal church in his community. After relating this specific confession he was told to remain after church and to double up on all his prayers. He said, "I got into more trouble for going to another church then sinning throughout the entire week.

Well, being young and fresh from the streets of Browning we rebelled against those "sour saints" and continued to have fun, laugh, and enjoy life. By the way our Pastor said it was all right to meet in our home for those of you who were wonder his position. If I had any wisdom at that time of my life I would have asked them to join us. Maybe that's all they really wanted.

The Bible says the rain falls on the just and un-just alike and when it dose we think that isn't fair since we are more spiritual or we have served the Lord longer than anyone else but when you think of it the rain is good for all. I am reminded of a time I was traveling with my Pastor friend from Spokane, Washington back to Browning. We were about 15 miles out from Sand Point, Idaho traveling at a high speed well past the speed limit.

Now in those early days our prayer for "traveling mercy" went something like this, "Lord Blind the eyes of the Highway Patrol so they will leave us alone oh yes, keep your hand upon us and keep us safe this day in Jesus name. Amen." Don't ask me who taught that prayer to me but it had to be an older Christian since we never prayed for mercy during our trips as sinners. Looking back it would have been easier to have just bought a radar detector, then blinding innocent police officers with my prayers.

As I stated my Pastor friend was leading as we whizzed around each corner and pushed on the gas peddle through the strait lanes as if we were NASCAR drivers. Just as we hung a tight right hand curve I noticed a black and white Idaho State Trooper vehicle ready to leap on us…I had no time to slow it down all I could think of is "Jesus help me."

When it was all said and done the officer gave me a ticket for a large amount that would help fill the Idaho State coffers. By the way did I mention that my Pastor, yes he was my Pastor at the time and he was my friend continued to put as much distance between him and me as the trooper "blessed me."

In my defense I asked the state trooper why he didn't stop both of us and ticket both of us. His reply was, "You were driving the fastest looking car (Pontiac Trans Am)...tell you what, why don't you catch up with your partner and have him share the ticket with you." I later told my friend what the state trooper said and all he could do was laugh and laugh and laugh. After I was able to talk with him I said the Bible really is true. How's that he said? Jesus is a friend that sticks closer than a brother, I told him. When you saw that cop all I had was Jesus, you were long gone.

The songwriter wrote a song with these words "This joy that I have the world didn't give it to me, the world didn't give it and the world can't take it away." Joy is part of the package of salvation David said in Psalms 51:12, "Restore unto me the joy of your salvation; and uphold me with your free spirit." The Holy Spirit has the ability to restore joy back into our lives as we confess our sin before God and let Him carry our burdens.

The opposite of joy is depression, condemnation, and the inability to know the will of God. In 2 John 12 he says, "...that our joy may be full." Nehemiah went a step further to express the source of our strength and said, "...For the joy of the Lord is your strength." (Nehemiah 8:10)

There have been times in my life I didn't feel like praising the Lord, but I did and I begin to experience the "Joy of the Lord." I have come to realize I can't have someone pray joy into me…joy comes from within a person. As I praise the Lord spiritual walls come tumbling down, bondages are broken, and strongholds must give way to the power of the Holy Ghost as I bless the name of Jesus. Psalms 150:6, "Let everything that has breath praise the Lord. Praise ye the Lord." You see this common thread throughout the book of Psalms beginning with chapter one, verse one; Jesus is called the "Blessed Man" and worthy to be praised.

Life at times can be very cruel and unpredictable; living on an Indian reservation you see this on a daily basis. I remember sometime back reading in the Great Falls Tribune about a community 90 miles northeast of Browning where they had lost a young person to an untimely accident that left the whole community in disbelief and confusion. The story of this young man made the front page for more than a week in this major Montana newspaper.

The synopsis of the story was how the community was powerless to deal with the extreme grief resulting from the death. I thought how different our communities were and that death on the Blackfeet reservation is a weekly ordeal and this is without exaggeration. At times they're maybe three to four bodies laying in wake some because of natural causes, others because of cancer, drug and alcohol, violent crimes, or an epidemic of diabetes that has swept over Indian Country reminisces to the smallpox that devastated entire tribes of the 1800's.

As a matter of fact from October 1, 2011 through January 10, 2012 I officiated eight funerals one after the other which left me exhausted and physically drained yet it was necessary to minister to the fullest extent of the Gospel as family after family approached me seeking comfort and direction during this time of tragedy in their life. After the death a "Promise Keeper" buddy I just stayed away from his funeral wake because I was tired. My prayer eventually was, "God please stop the dying in our land. Stop the pain that has overshadowed our people."

We witness more death in a month on the Blackfeet reservation than most people see in a lifetime. In most cases if I'm not officiating a funeral on our reservation I'm doing the music. Without the strength of the Holy Spirit a person would yield to depression, anger, or any number of negative emotional reactions.

Many Indian communities do not have the privilege to heal so we continue with "unresolved grief" that hinder our life from moving forward. One week you're laying a loved one to rest and then a few weeks or months down the road you repeat the process over again with another close friend, relative, or family member. I often tell the people, "The only way to really heal and move forward is to allow Jesus into their life. He is the only one who can give true peace." Sorrow and grief is natural however, prolong grief becomes a tool the enemy uses to bring sickness and defeat into your life. We must recognize the difference and give no place to the devil according to scripture.

Many a times I have spoken at wakes and funeral services of our tribal members whose families are reaching out for hope during a time of utter darkness and in those moments I pray asking God to give me the wisdom and courage to speak hope back into their fragile existence. I often sing a song that I wrote some years ago with these words, "Thou art worthy to be praised O' Lord. When I'm down in the valley so low or the mountain way up high, I'm going to lift my hands toward heaven and praise your name, thou art worthy to be praised."

Today a young man stopped me in the grocery store and shared with me how he was blessed by the words I had spoken at a recent funeral. As I drove back home I begin to give thanks to the Lord because it is God who really was speaking I just offered up my voice. My desire is to continue to serve my community, my reservation, and my people through the Word of God for without a preacher how shall they know? The message I preach is that God offers grace and hope if only we ask.

Jesus went among the people and prayed for them. He sat down at their dinner tables at ate with them; he even stood by the graveside and weep because of the loose of a dear friend. If ever there was an example to follow, it is Jesus. So each time I'm asked to assist our people I'm reminded of how Jesus changed life after life because of His character and ability to look beyond our human fault and failure and see just the need. He was moved with compassion and love, mercy and grace, peace and joy…even on the cross he looked into the future and saw you and me in need of a Savior. We all need Jesus

CHAPTER EIGHT

One More Mountain to Climb, One More Valley to Cross

My wife Muriel often reminds me that I have a "Pastor's Heart" and will leave the 99 in search of the one lost sheep. I am reminded of my father who minister in the same fashion. One time he was ministering on another Indian reservation in southern Montana and according to my mother each service witnessed an increase from the Holy Spirit.

It was during one of these services he noticed and minister friend who he had not seen in many years sitting in the back of the church as if not wanting to be noticed. As was my dads natured he invited the minister to share the platform with the rest of the Pastors and such. After much encouragement that lost sheep surrendered to the request of my dad and sat on the platform.

Yes my father knew this man was away from God for many years but yet he loved him as a friend...as a brother in the Lord. He didn't embarrass this former preacher in any demeaning way. He didn't try and prophecy over him concerning condemnation and any other such foolishness, he just befriended him with the love of Jesus.

Within this same meeting that man rededicated his life to Jesus Christ and begin to follow the Lord yet in a greater way. This man later testified that it was my father's invitation to sit on the platform that renewed his HOPE in Jesus. He told the crowd how he had felt rejected and abandoned by the Christian community after his failure to stay committed to the Christian walk. He described the hardness of his heart toward those who had wronged him and his family and within the same service he was grateful for the opportunity to know the goodness of the Lord again because one man had the insight and courage to show him kindness. Wow! That is powerful example of Christ working in our life.

That man later became a Pastor and established a work in his community, he has since passed on to be with the Lord since the Bible says, "To be absent from the body is to be present with the Lord." Isn't that a blessing? He died in the Lord rather than in the world as a sinner. I understand his daughter now is the Pastor of the church. This is a rich heritage to leave to your children and a great testimony of God's grace.

There is a song I have written that says, "I will worship you O Lord, I will worship you. When I'm down in the valley or the mountain way up high, I'm going to lift my hands toward heaven and worship you Lord." I sing this song realizing that there will be valleys and mountains in my life and the same applies to you. Some of you are going through spiritual storms that have shipped wreaked you and shaken your spiritual foundation but you must hold on. It isn't always going to be dark and stormy. We serve the God of breakthrough, the God of the Mountains (El~Shaddai) or "Almighty God." He is El~Roi "God who sees me." He is Yahweh~Shammah "The Lord is there." When I don't know what to pray I just whisper His name and the atmosphere begins to change. At the sound of His voice, the wind will cease to blow. All creation become subject unto Him. Peace be still, know that I'm God.

"I'm Not Ready to Die"

Not long ago I endured one of the most trying times of my life as sickness had taken hold of my body and I was under a continuous attack of pain throughout my lower back and left leg, soon weight loss was evident since I lost my desire to eat. Doctor visit after doctor visit resulted in the same, no cure. At first I was able to endure in my own strength but soon after I was reaching out to anything that would relieve the pain. Of course the doctors were throwing all types of medication at me, which only worsen the problem.

For six months my bed was the living room floor, I could not lay in a bed. I could not ride for long periods in the car. Worst of all I could not sleep. Lack of sleep and perpetual pain are the body's worst enemy. The pain pushed aside my desire to read the Bible because I could not focus for long periods of time. Hour after hour was this wave of discomfort with no end in sight. Without rest for the body our mind enters an emotional roller coaster that cuts at your very soul.

Each Sunday I would muster up the strength to minister at Four Winds Assembly of God church since we were the Pastors. The most amazing thing would happen, as the anointing would cover me …the pain would diminish and I would become my former self. This amazed me each and every time to witness the power of God over my life. As time progressed it became more difficult to even get dressed. One Sunday I tried my hardest to accomplish this task only to fail that is when my wife said, "Bill I'll minister today."

I promised God I would never pray this but one evening all alone in my house laying on the floor I said, "Please God, pity me, take this suffering from me." During this time I begin to search myself just like Job of old. Where did I go wrong? I'm I praying correctly? Do I need to forgive anyone? On and on and on I searched my heart. As the ministers on television would come on and announce they were ready to pray I would do whatever was asked of me. Stand-up, touch the screen, put your hand on the place that is hurting you. If they had said stand on your head and give a special offering I probably would have done that also. I had everyone that I knew praying for me.

One day the Holy Spirit quicken me and said, "Bill, pray for yourself just as you have prayed for others." I looked at my hands and said these hands are anointed because of the Holy Ghost. I have seen God do wonders and yes-even miracles in my lifetime so I begin to pray. I became a spiritual pit-bull and would not let go of those words. Shortly after that I was in a motel room sleeping on the floor, as Muriel was in the bedroom however this night was different.

The entire living-room became pitch black with darkness and for a moment fear tried to overtake me I found myself leaving my body entering a place of utter darkness unable to pull myself back. In that moment I had given up, I was tried of fighting; I was tired of praying…asking and asking and asking with no results. I thought in a few minutes it will be all over and I won't have to suffer any more. Looking back I knew what was happening and I didn't care that I was dying because I couldn't fight death on my own.

And He said unto me, My Grace is sufficient for thee: for my strength is made perfect in weakness (2 Corinthians 12:9). This scripture became a reality to me for suddenly I cried out in my spirit, **"I'm not ready to die."** Before me flashed pictures of my children, grandchildren, and my wife. The love I have for them would not allow me to go. I refused to go. I said there are places I, still want to go and preach, there are souls I want to reach and as quickly as those words came forth I was pulled back into my body.

The entire room was filled with a light I can't describe yet there was this awesome peace and for the first time in months I sat up in a chair and begin to worship God. I wept as His presence filled the room, filled my life once again. I felt so wonderful just to praise him with all of my heart. This all happen around three o'clock in the morning and I could not wait for Muriel to awake so we could venture back to Browning, I just knew that the trial, test, call it what you may was coming to an end.

That Sunday morning as I waited for the congregation to arrive the Holy Spirit gave me a song, which I sing at every opportunity since it declared what God meant to me through it all. "I have no sad story to tell, I can't complain. God you been so good to me, God you been so good to me. You gave me joy, you gave peace, and you even let me smile again, God you been so good to me. You saved my soul, you made me whole, you put my feet on the Rock to stay, God you been so good to me…so good, so good, God you been so good to me."

You see it is when I came to the weakest point in my life and I had no control His strength and Mercy rose up to declare His Majesty, His love over my life. What a mighty God we serve and He just gets better and better every day. Choose to trust God. The best songs I have ever written were when I was in my spiritual wilderness. The best messages from the Holy Spirit were when I was in my valley of decision.

I have discovered that through spiritual pressing there is produced a greater anointing in my life. Genesis 50:24-25 Joseph said, "God will surely visit you…"I fall down on my knees, O' Lord and pray. That you keep me strong when life's storms come my way. My heart I give to you, my life is in your hand. I give you all I'm O' Lord, on my knees I pray. Broken and alone, I stand before your throne. My heart I give to you, my life is in your hand." When Delilah probed Samson she was symbolic of the devil "testing us" for our weak areas. My weak area is I love to Praise the name of Jesus!

CHAPTER NINE

This Too Shall Pass

I believe the biggest surprise for most new Christians is that they think after coming to Christ all their troubles are over, which is far from the truth or just their ignorance concerning the Word of God. It is these same individuals that soon become disheartened in the Lord and begin to look back into the past for answers. You cannot resolve spiritual conflicts with carnal weapons. The Bible says, "For the weapons of our warfare are not carnal, but mighty through God to the pulling down of strongholds (II Corinthians 4:10)."

Our walk with God is about warfare in the spiritual realm. The King of kings and the Lord of lords called us soldiers, warriors, over comers, men of valor and virtuous woman! When God delivered the children of Israel from the bondage of Egypt, He provided them with leadership, direction, and purpose however, when the first 'trials and test' came there way discontentment blurred their vision, and fear destroyed their 'season of opportunity.'

Faith is about taking one step at a time. Faith is calling those things which are not as if they were. Faith will cause you to rise up in the midst of the enemy and proclaim your position in Jesus Christ. If I'm called a different name by a stranger I can contest it because I know who I am. My name isn't Bob, Bud, or Brad Smith. My name is Bill Old Chief and I know where I come from and who my people are, the same is with my position in Christ. I know who my heavenly Father is. I know what Jesus has done for me. I know what God called me for. I like to say it this way, "Devil, go lie to someone who isn't covered with the blood of Jesus."

When I came to the church alter and accepted Jesus into my life I became an heir and joint heir (Galatians 3:29) into the kingdom of God. I now have the right to call Him Father and He calls me son (Galatians 4:6). If the devil is telling you different set him straight and remind him your name is now written in Lambs Book of Life and you are covered with the Blood of Jesus he has no right in your life or calling you something different. Your past is under the Blood of Jesus.

When others see giants and walled cities faith will find a way through every obstacle. It isn't our feelings that will move the hand of God it is our faith. Crying over the past will never produce healing or victory just tears on your pillow. Psalms 34:19 says, "Many are the afflictions of the righteous: but the Lord delivered him out of them all." The children of Israel wandered for forty-years because of their unbelief and disobedience. Forty-years is a generation. Sometimes we become captives of our past and instead of moving forward in the things of God we retreat every time someone says we can't live a victorious life in Jesus. By the way the journey should have only taken 13 days.

I have come to realize that all things are possible through Christ Jesus. I don't evaluate my success on the failures of others or if I have gone a greater spiritual distance than my father. Each morning that I wake I thank God for His "Grace." I thank Him for His mercy. David said it best, "When my feet begin to slip, your mercy held me up." I start each day because of the breath of God in my lungs. Genesis 2:7 says, "And the Lord God formed man from the dust of the ground, and breathed into his nostrils the breath of life; and man became a living soul."

Considering my status as a Native American male I have every right to be angry. I can convince myself "I have the right to blame others" for my shortcomings, setbacks, and lack of opportunities or I can begin to see the God given potential within myself. God has given me the ability to think, reason, and decide my future. If I live in disparity it isn't because someone is holding me down, it is because I choose not to move from my present condition. The world has a saying, "Don't you have the sense to come in out of the rain?"

We live in a time of opportunity according to Proverbs 9:9, "Give instruction to a Wiseman, and he will be yet wiser; teach a just man, and he will increase in learning." Proverbs 4:7 says, "Wisdom is the principle thing, therefore get wisdom: and with all thy getting get understanding." Ignorance isn't a racial thing... it is a personal thing.

"Faith"

James 2:26 "Faith without works is dead." What is James saying here? In verse fourteen James says what profit is it if a man says he has faith but has no works. Then James continues that if we encounter a person who is naked and in need of food and ignore their condition by sending them on their way with just saying "Bless you" we miss the point or the opportunity to witness true faith and God's love in our life.

I often tell people that faith and fear grow in the exact manner... we feed them by our actions. Fear is just a word until I feed it with my emotions that create an atmosphere of panic, uncertainty, and stress. As an example someone will relate a chilling incident that happened to him or her one stormy night as the power was cut off and there were no lights. Soon they heard voices, furniture begin to move, and voices came from the cute little pup. Low and behold, you experience a similar storm and the lights go out all of a suddenly your mind begins to race...what was that? Did that object move? Was my dog talking? Your emotions are out of control and the devil is using that opportunity to fill your spirit with fear and torment (1 John 4:18).

As a sinner I never knew what faith was or the importance in plays within our life. As a matter of fact the Bible says it is impossible to please God without faith..."for he who comes to God must believe that He is, and that He is a rewarder of them who diligently seek Him." My faith and your faith has one source. "So then Faith comes by hearing, and hearing by the Word of God." The Word of God when applied to our life will produce FAITH.

As an immature Christian most of my time was spent in the spiritual valleys of life and just like others I would ask God, "Why?" As a seasoned minister I still valley walk from time to time however, it is with a different mindset. I don't see it as punishment or a downgrade in promotion it is where I discover what God can truly do in my life.

The Bible says, "When a man's way pleases God he maketh even his enemies to be at peace with him. Now that's a powerful indicator to our position in Christ. When a former enemy blesses you or helps you know that your ways or actions are pleasing to God.

Right and wrong thinking will determine your outcome in life it is simple as that and it begins with the simplest things around us. Sometime back I entered a woman's house unannounced and she was totally surprised by my visit. Her first words were if I knew you were coming I would have cleaned my house. Well I paid her a visit again one year later and guess what her words were? Everything appeared as if I never left the room. She had good intentions of cleaning her house but for whatever reason it just never happened.

Christians ensnare themselves by the words they speak as I stated before, "Life and death are in the words we speak according to the Word of God." Have you ever meet some one with a great personality and you just enjoyed yourself with them for the first five minutes then all of a sudden they transform and their conversation becomes contaminated and unpleasant? Their dirty little secrets and past offences fester in your mind long after you have departed leaving you feeling contaminated and in want of a shower. Wrong thinking and negative words will produce three things in your life, which are: daily struggles, oppression, and a wounded spirit. You can speak in tongues, read your Bible, and go to church weekly but if you cannot control the words that come from your mouth they will come back and haunt you every time.

Apostle Paul tells us it is a "flesh problem" and that we must mortify (Romans 8:13) the deeds of the flesh. In another part James says that the tongue is like a ship without a rudder or a horse without a bridle (James 3:3-5)…both are uncontrollable and will cause injury and damage if gone unchecked. It's so easy to get caught up in the snare of gossip and deceit under the false intent of, "I just told you this so you could pray about it." You know what, the Holy Spirit still speaks into my spirit and leads me concerning the needs of the body of Christ and if prayer is needed I will obey the Lord but I don't need to hear the trash of gossip in order to pray.

Most problems in our lives could be corrected if we just kept our mouth closed. The saddest picture is someone who has been saved for a number of years living in defeat. Recently a woman asked for prayer and her request was, "Please pray for my grandchildren's salvation." I thought to myself twenty-nine years ago she was asking that same request only it was for her children. As I looked at her in the church service she was still seated by herself content with just the crumbs that were falling from the spiritual table in her life.

Like Joshua and Caleb who said we could take the land, I can't sit back and be content with just crumbs. God has promised so much to us as His children. Were living in a season of "Divine Opportunities" and great expectation. There is a stirring within me that

Says "get ready." Joshua told the children of Israel, "In the morning were crossing over." Its time to step into your blessing, into your destiny, into your future. Everywhere that the sole of your feet touch God will give it to you. The songwriter said, "I'm taking it back, everything the devil stole from me I'm taking it back."

Stepping into Your Future...

Wow, that sounds so easy. Before I became a Christian I considered myself just another "Indian boy from the rez." Words like future, purpose, and destiny were foreign to me as a trip to the moon as they say. They were not part of my vocabulary. My days before my conversion were filled with uncertainty and wishful thinking. For three years my sinner buddies and I planned on traveling to the "Missoula Kegger" for a party of a lifetime that is only four hours away. We never did make it my vision couldn't even take me four hours down the road. The Bible teaches that without a vision we will perish (die) and according to statistics from the state of Montana during that time as a Native American male I should have been dead or in prison. However, God had other plans for me that would later amaze me beyond belief.

Consider Joseph who went from the "PIT" (Prophet in Training) to the throne room and David who cared for the sheep would later lead a nation as their king. Often times when we are in our sinful nature or in a realm of disparity we can see no further than our existing need. Over and over you will look in the mirror and see failure because of sin. Ten of the twelve spies that were sent out by Moses into the Promise Land could only see the struggles of life before them and refused to believe the Word of God concerning their destiny. Both Caleb and Joshua said, "We can take the land" because they had a different spirit. When others saw giant problems, they saw giant opportunities.

My world changed forever at the age of twenty-three on May 21,1980, around 10 p.m. this was the night that I attended a small Pentecostal church in Browning, Montana with a hand full of individuals including my wife Muriel as I literally ran to the alter asking God to forgive me and to change me. I wasn't looking for riches or fame, only freedom from the pains of my past. I wanted to be a better father and a better husband and I couldn't achieve this on my own. I wanted a better future for my family.

I often tell people that my life begin because of Jesus. I didn't have any minister or prophet speak words concerning my destiny, it begin to flow forth out of my spirit as I sought God in my prayer closet each day after work. My future became clear as I surrendered myself to the leading of the Holy Spirit in my times of fasting and prayer. I became so hungry for God that nothing else mattered except having fellowship with Him daily. The Word of God declares in Psalm 23, "Give us this day our daily bread."

I wasn't content with spiritual leftovers...I needed to hear from God regarding Bill Old Chief and it was in this season of searching that I realized I was called of God to minister to others whether it was one on one or before thousands. I didn't ask God for a position or title, in reality I felt so insignificant in His presence I would just say, "More of you Lord and less of me." As a matter of fact I cleaned the church for the first two years week after week without question or pay because I was so thankful concerning my salvation and that I had a place to call "my church."

Looking back, many of the young people that accepted Christ during that season had ambitions to minister from the pulpit. David said that I might be just a doorkeeper in the house of God. Often times when we look to promote ourselves we miss out completely concerning the leading of the Holy Spirit and then we begin to blame God for the many mistakes and failures that disobedience produces. Many of the young people of that time would not clean the church or restrooms because it was below them. They did not commit to a local church. They were not faithful in their giving, and many are not serving God today.

Sometimes stepping into your future may involve taking out the trash before you have the ability to cast out an evil spirit. It may involve giving of yourself, before others give to you. It may require listening rather than talking. The songwriter said, "If you want to be great in God's kingdom you must learn to be a servant to all."

As a young Christian I discovered I loved to pray and later I learned how to fast and what the purpose of a fast was. It was during these times in prayer that would last for hours I connected with God. The hunger to know Him kept me coming back for more. My prayer time wasn't about creating a great ministry or name for myself; I just wanted to know God. That may sound strange considering the time we live in everyone wants to be a star and recognized, why do you think YouTube and Face Book are so popular?

It was during this period that I begin to experience what I thought were strange events in my life however, I trusted the Holy Spirit to lead me and guide me into all truth. The first experience involved an "open vision" as I prayed just before our evening service. I could open my eyes or close them and the vision was before me. As the Spirit of God came upon me heavily I could see this young man walking in deep depression (I felt the depression in my spirit) along a city street. The vision was so vivid the very cracks in the sidewalk appeared to leap at me. I noticed that the roots of the large trees were pushing the sidewalk up in certain sections and I thought for a moment the person would stumble because of the shoes he had on. The entire street had the old style "Victorian houses" with iron rod or white picket fences.

This young man was dressed in a silk shirt with flower prints and white bell-bottom jeans. His black hair was lying on his shoulders and he had platform shoes on. I watched him walk for about half a block in the darkness with his back to me, and then he turned to face me, immediately I recognized him and called out his name. The thing is I hadn't seen him since we were children given that he lived in another state but still I was able to recognize him in this condition. Then the Lord spoke these words, "Tell his parents I am going to save Jr." His parents were holding a weeklong meeting at our church and this was the last night that they were going to be there.

Fear filled me, I had never seen anything like this or was I ever asked to relay a message for the Lord. I was afraid that they would laugh at me or just rebuke me for "acting so spiritual." At this point I begin to negotiate with God and said, "If they are parked at the church when I get there I'll tell them." When I arrived at the church they were the only car there. I built up enough courage and asked if I could talk with them. I described what I had seen and before I could say any more the mother said, "That's my son... that's Jr." I then told them Jesus was going to save him within a month. As I departed their vehicle both parents were in tears.

Some years later that entire family ministered at the church I was Pastoring and they reminded me of the word I delivered to them, by the way Jr. was ministering with them as a part of their ministry team he had given his life to the Lord within a month of their return to Washington State. He continues to serve the Lord today as a husband and father.

The next event that I witnessed happened in the early morning hours, I would say around three o'clock in the morning to be specific. I was wakening from a dead sleep to see our bedroom filled with a bright light however; the light was coming from the outside. The reason this was bizarre we lived in the country about fifteen miles west of Browning and the nearest house was more than a mile away plus we had no security light...just the stars.

I felt no fear so I assumed this was a Godly matter. I looked to my left and realized Muriel was still sleeping so I slowly got out of bed and went to the window to explore what was the source of the light. To my amazement there was a perfect circle of light about 200 feet wide. It wasn't like a flashlight that disperses being bright in the center and weaker toward the outside, this light was the same brightness as if a towering wall.

The only way I can describe the light as "being pure." Every blade of grass was standing strait up, there was no sound, no wind just the light. I looked upward wondering if I could see the source but it appeared to be a pillar of light hundreds of feet tall. To this day I have not seen a man made light to compare with it.

I turned to look at Muriel again and even called her name…she did not respond. I remember telling myself, "I am I dreaming?" And the answer was no! This lasted for about ten minutes. I kept waiting for something to happen or to see something and just as suddenly as the light appeared it was gone.

I could now see the stars that filled the northern sky near our home against the Rocky Mountain front. I waited for instruction for the Holy Spirit but none came so I just got back into bed and fell asleep. I often ponder what the significance of this encounter was and can only conclude that angels were watching over us and I caught a glimpse of them while on duty.

A Fast for the Blackfeet Nation

My third God encounter involved fasting for a long period of time over four consecutive years. As we were nearing the close of one year and about to begin a new I felt the unction of the Holy Spirit calling me to fast. I shared this with Muriel and explained what I was about to do, with this she asked me how long I would be gone, my reply was, "When I get hungry I'll be back" and I was serious. Up to this point I had never fasted or even considered what it entailed.

To make a long story short my strategy was to find an isolated place and take only water with me...water only was the plan however, I never planned on fasting during the month of January in Northern Montana, which is the coldest month of the year. Rather than fight the Holy Spirit concerning the time frame I ventured north where the hills touch the mountains and for three days I prayed day and night calling upon God to heal our land and raise forth leaders who would stand in the gap for the Blackfeet people.

Again the next year the same feeling came upon me and I knew what was being asked of me. This time I fasted for seven days, praying day and night and drinking only water. For those wondering how I kept warm I had insulated coveralls and blankets to wrap myself with against the bitter cold January nights. Also my prayer remained the same...God heal our land and rise up leaders with a backbone to fight for the Blackfeet people.

The third year I fasted ten days and then on the fourth year I fasted fifteen-days straight. I remember during the nights because of my location high upon the hills I could see the lights in all the communities on the Blackfeet Indian reservation. To quote a man of God, "It was as if heaven bowed low to touch my spirit." Now understand me: I never heard any voices. I never saw anything unusual. All I experienced was the presence of the Holy Spirit. It was as if God was cleaning me out and filling me with His "Spirit of Revelation." What I didn't realize was God was directing my life in a manner I could not imagine possible. Looking back I would consider myself to be like David in the backside of the dessert watching over the sheep. David had no ideal that he was being prepared for kingdom matters.

All through this process my prayer was that God would rise up Godly men who would have the courage and wisdom to lead the Blackfeet people. A person who had a heart for the people. Soon after the conclusion of my fast I was asked by a friend, "How do we take back our land from the enemy?" My reply was according to Joshua 1:3, when God told Joshua every place that the sole of your foot shall walk upon, that have I given to you. Joshua continues to say, within three days you shall pass over the Jordan River and possess the land, which the Lord God gave unto you.

This word quicken us and we decided to gather as many men from the different churches on the reservation that would heed what the Spirit of God was directing and canvas our reservation with prayer. Thirty days from that point we were gathered 39 strong. One Pastor from the Methodist Church. One Pastor from the Baptists Church. One representative from the Catholic Church and myself as Pastor of Community Christian Fellowship. The remaining men where from each church mentioned. Considering the number 39 in retrospect it is the same number of lashes upon the back of Jesus for our healing...we were asking for the healing of our land.

We decided the best way to cover our reservation effectively was to go in four directions. Our mandate was to stop and pray as directed by the Holy Spirit where we felt there was a land dispute, racial prejudice, death on the highway because of alcohol or drugs, ancient spirits the were holding our people captive to superstitions, and just healing for our land according to II Chronicles 7:14, "If my people, which are called by my name, shall humble themselves, and pray, and seek my face, and turn from their wicked ways; then will I hear from heaven, and will forgive their sin, and will heal their land."

That afternoon I witnessed 39 men who shed tears in a public place as occupants of cars curious passed by wondering what these men were up to in front of our Blackfeet Tribal Government complex. We had one objective on our minds as we stood unified around the flagpole and that was to pray! We had no agenda or time frame rather we just let the Holy Spirit lead us and each man prayed according in that fashion.

As I stood with the rest of the men I saw a vision for a brief moment, which lasted less, then 10 seconds. However in that instant I saw myself in a specific office that I had visited with my dad when I was the age of 13. I saw the pictures of dignitaries hanging throughout the room that was about 20'x 35'. I saw a round conference table where meetings were held and I remember there was another group of men holding hands while they prayed.

After returning home I was troubled by the vision and shared the experience with my wife. I described everything exactly as I saw it in the vision and I told her that office was the Chairman of our tribe or as some would say the "Chief." I didn't even know if that office still existed since it had been so many years since visiting our Chairman with my dad. Without hesitation she said, "Bill, you're going to be the next Chairman of our tribe." Wow! To those that are unfamiliar with tribal government that is like saying 'you're the next President of the United States…it has that same corresponding elements.

"Watch what you pray for"

Now as they say "What's the rest of the story?" Soon after this vision I was approached by three different individuals at different times who all shared the exact message, "Bill, you need to run for tribal council." The problem was I had never run for anything in my life except the dinner table. I never even talked tribal politics yet; their words reverberated deep within my soul. Is this the will of God for my life? Is it all right for a Christian to serve in a public office? What about my family…what about my job?

Like a puzzle, I begin to put the pieces together and try and make sense of what was happening in my life. Why would seemly disconnect strangers be talking to me about serving on our tribal council? At the time it seemed too unreasonable a request to ask of me considering the responsibility that position carries. So like a good husband I talked it over with my wife who could put things into perspective from the worst of situations. Her final statement was, "If this is what God is calling you to do then I'll stand with you, pray with you, and support you until the finish."

Still the uncertainly persisted in my heart, this is truly a step of faith I would be embarking upon. I'm a strong believer that you can't go back, you can't live it over again and if I was to accept this "season of opportunity" then it meant resigning from my position as Native American Coordinator and Work Leader / Equipment Engineer Operator for the east side roads department with the National Park Service where I had served for 17 years. Maybe some of you have traveled down this crossroad of life not knowing what tomorrow holds.

Some days later a man from Great Falls was passing through Browning and wanted to meet with me for a couple of hours, so I accepted his invitation thinking it would be nice to talk about ministry things other than tribal politics and the decision that lay ahead of me. When it was all said and done this man ministered to every question I had put before God and the thing about it we didn't even discuss what I was going through, it was something he had gone through three years before and a major decision he had to make that would effect all that was important to him.

I just listen in amazement thinking how God used my time of fasting, the group of men to pray for our reservation, the three men who asked me to run for tribal government, and now this person who was pouring out his heart yet, it was if I was speaking face to face with God and He was instructing me point by point, line upon line. At that specific point in time I made up my mind and said yes Lord! That man never knew the impact he made on me with the words he spoke into my heart that warm spring afternoon on our "Government Square" directly across from the tribal complex and the office I would occupy within a matter of months as the Blackfeet Nation Tribal Chairman.

Proverbs 29:2, "When the righteous are in authority, the people rejoice: but when the wicked beareth rule, the people mourn." The word mourn in this passage is exactly that of mourning because a death of a loved one. Evil rulers put a hardship on the people. I often say the people are a reflection of the leadership. Consider your household, your company or place of employment...now how about the leadership within the United States, state government, or tribal government. "The trouble with most Christians is, they know what is happening, but they don't know what's going on."

What is happening behind the spiritual scene is more important than what is happening before our natural eye. As a young Christian we encounter temptation, trials, and tests that appear colossal at the time and un-winnable in our inadequate human strength. One such test proved to be a coming out for me and strengthen my faith in the God I serve.

In my days as a "Prodigal Son" I had the ability to take care of myself if you know what I mean. I never went looking for trouble however, if pushed I would take care business and in most cases emerge as the victor. Now the town I grew up in was and is a tough town and any sign of weakness will eventually be the demise of your existence with countless scares to show for it.

Shortly after my conversion I went with my daughter Karrilyn who was four-years at the time to retrieve a horse bridle that I had loaned to an individual. Immediately I realized something was wrong since the person had a very bad attitude toward me as if I had done some thing wrong in asking for my property. The reason the yellow flags went up was this man would have never talked to me in this manner when I wasn't a Christian.

What happened next took only seconds as I became tried of his tone of voice toward me. I was standing outside of a corral and he was on the inside, as I reached up and forward to

get on his side of the corral he grabbed a 2x4 from the ground and hit me over the head. The moment I realized I was bleeding I rushed toward him with extreme force and was about to use my fist on his face.

Absolute fear filled his face realizing he had crossed the line by hitting me. I didn't care that I was saved or what people would say about me. My old nature rose up and I was going to make him pay for what he had done to me in front of my daughter. Within an inch from his face my fist stopped as if from some unseen force… it just rested in midair for a few seconds and then I spoke these words, "Hitting you isn't worth my Salvation" and then I slowly walked away.

I wasn't praising God or thanking Him that I had passed the "test." That evening I was in the bedroom of my father and mother and relayed what had happened. For a brief moment I though my parents were going to call down fire from heaven to destroy this person and have the birds of prey eat his flesh to the bone, but it was just the opposite. The words my father spoke struck me to the core of my soul. He said, "Bill, you haven't even got your feet wet yet. You will face many more heartbreaking tests and trials however, never think God has forsaken you."

Those words persist within my life just like those of the Drill Instructors who helped me get through basic training in the United States Army. If I could have seen how God was going to use that moment in my life for the good I would have rejoiced. Joseph said that which was intended for evil God turned into a blessing.

Some months later I was with my Pastor in Poplar, Montana on the Fort Peck Indian Reservation. I was his official driver slash gopher. I was enjoying the trip, fellowship, and nightly services until my Pastor said, "Bill Saturday night you will be preaching." This stopped me in my tracks since I thought he was kidding. But he wasn't. Your ready and this is the place for you to step forward. I went into an instance fast not because the Holy Spirit told me but because of fear.

I never dreamed I would be ministering outside of the local church let alone to a full house. The moment I took the microphone it felt as if the entire world was on my back. It became hard to breath and sweat flowed from my forehead as if I was standing under a waterfall. The words just would not come out correctly let alone make any sense. This embarrassment seemed to last an eternity and all I could say was, "Jesus help me." I thought at any moment they would begin to throw rotten fruit at me. But as they say, "Experience is the best teacher."

Suddenly the Holy Spirit spoke to me, "Tell them what happen to you when you got hit on the head." Just like in the movies, time stopped and an eerie silence filled the room. Courage spilling over in my heart and conviction flowed from my lips; I shared with them my experience. It seemed the entire church was crying so I called for an "alter call" (that's what all the big preachers do) and to my surprise the front of the church was completely full. People wanted salvation or to rededicate their life back to God while others wanted healing.

The last person I prayed with was a nine-year-old girl who was crying uncontrollable. I got on my knees beside her and asked her what she needed from the Lord. My grandmother can't walk and I want her to walk. It was as if someone had thrown a cold bucket of water on me or being hit all over again with the 2x4 on my head...I was stunned. I didn't know what to do. Music was blasting, people dancing and rejoicing, just when I thought I had the victory and the service was about to end...now this.

I turned to my Pastor who was singing and made the expression with my hands lifted upward, "What do I do?" He just motioned to me to continue and smiled. Again I prayed, "Jesus what do I do, I can't heal anyone." In that moment I recalled the scripture, "So be it unto your faith." Once again courage rushed through my being and excitement filled my heart for what God was about to do. Little girl do you believe your grandmother is going to walk? Smiling ear to ear she said YES! Since you believe so will I, then we prayed.

The next night being the last nigh the church was filling quickly and once again here comes that little nine-year-old girl crying. My first thought was, "Her grandmother died." She wraps her arms around me and begins to tell the story.

This morning I woke up and someone was cooking breakfast. I could smell the bacon, eggs, and coffee so I raced from my bed into the kitchen to find my grandmother standing over the stove. As I'm hugging her she turns and says, "This is my grandmother." She didn't look weak or feeble as a matter of fact she looked very strong.

I thought if I had reacted negatively that day months ago when the man hit me over the head this woman would have never received her healing in my inaugural ministry moment. God used something evil to bring goodness forth in a total stranger hundreds of miles away. That same love was given to you and I as Jesus gave his life on the cross the Bible says, Obedience is better than sacrifice." It's easy to strike back at those who oppose you or speak against you however, as a child of God learn to protect the anointing in your life since you pay a mighty price for it through self-sacrifice and submission to God. Just remember God will take care what belongs to Him, "Touch not my anointed or do my Prophets no harm."

Conclusion of the Matter

Two years after becoming a Christian I faced one of the biggest spiritual mountains of my life. I tell this story since it allows me to refocus and realize that God truly has my life in his hands. One of the most difficult times of my life was the loss of our baby daughter in a terrible accident. One moment we are enjoying a beautiful autumn morning and then the next I am holding the limp body of my daughter in my arms watching as my world collapses. The police actually had to forcibly take her from me as I fought to keep her in my arms. Everything seemed to stand still.

I could hear the voices of others around me trying to make sense of what had happen. I remember setting on the back steps of our small house that I had grown to love because it was so cozy for our little family and for a brief moment I heard the voice of the enemy saying, "You have every right to be angry. Go get drunk no one will hold it against you. Go ahead and leave your family look what God did to you after all you have done for Him."

It must have been a few minutes of this that I realized what was happening and the only thing I could do was quote the Word of God. I had no prayers to pray, since prayer appeared so far from my spirit. Tears had flooded my eyes and I couldn't cry anymore. But these words came forth in the depts of my heart, "The Lord giveth and the Lord taketh away blessed be the name of the Lord." Please don't judge me for quoting this verse to this day I can't tell you why the specific scripture came forth, it just did. I told the devil, "If ever there was a time my family needed me it was now."

In that moment I realized I would never be the same. In that moment I realized I had become a man at the age of twenty-five. My focused had shifted from me and my hurt to protecting Muriel and my other daughter Karrilyn. Before I had accepted Jesus into my life all I had known was failure. I never completed or finished anything that really made a difference. Whenever trouble came my way I would look for an escape in alcohol or drugs and then pay the consequences later. So when the Spirit of God rose up in me I realized we were going to make it because of Jesus.

Healing didn't happen over night as a matter of fact I mentioned to a minister friend during the wake period, "How can I ever tell people of the goodness of Jesus after what has happened to me? How can I ever preach again?" His reply was, "In due time the Word will come back and you won't have to rush in to it...let Jesus heal you."

Months and even years later I would hear people who wanted to encourage us say they had a dream of my daughter or they had a word from the Lord concerning her well being in heaven. Immediately I would close them out since I hadn't dreamed of her since her death. My thoughts were always, "Why would God share with them the preciousness of my daughter and not me?" To be honest with you I became very mad at God and those who wanted to do well. For twelve years after her death I would not mention her name and if anyone said her name I would walk out of the room.

> "Weeping May enduring for the night,
> but joy comes in the morning"

After sometime I begin to preach and minister throughout the country...but I wasn't healed I just learned to live with the loss by not mentioning her name or thinking about that dreadful morning. Everything that was associated with that day I buried including my daughter. Isn't amazing how we can wear our mask with a smile, yet cry inside.

About twelve years later in the late Fall just before the snow begin to fall I had a vision of my daughter Deanna. I was lying in my bedroom resting after a long day at work. Muriel was in the kitchen cooking supper and our other children were in their rooms. I was aware of everything throughout the house as I lay there and within moments I smelled the most overwhelming divine fragrance that just captured my attention.

In the vision my eyes were closed and I was in the middle of the "Oval" at the University of Montana in Missoula. Students were crossing from one direction to the other as they do during the end of classes. All of a sudden I noticed students beginning to run in fear as they looked upward toward the sky. This caused me to run also since there were three 'creatures' descending from the clouds.

Every time I ran in a particular direction the creatures would follow me all the while they became closer to me as they descended gently toward the ground. It was at this point I herd a female voice say, "Dad, it's me Deanna" and I stopped in my tracks turning slowly to see who had said this. There stood two large angels about seven and a half (7 ½) or eight feet tall. They appeared to be mighty warriors and their appearance resemble that of secret service agents that protect the United States President. I realized they were protecting a young lady about fourteen years of age. All three were dressed in white garments, hanging inches from the ground that seemed to shine without blinding the eyes.

Total peace engulfed me where fear once raced uncontrollably.

At that moment I realized no harm was going to come to her with protectors such as these. The angels never paid any attention to me throughout the entire encounter rather they continued to scan the "Oval" area with their eyes as if waiting for some expected intruder which never did arrive.

In the brief time that we spent talking she said, "Dad it's me Deanna, I am all right, everything is Ok." She continued to say she just came to let me know it wouldn't be long and we will be together again, <u>don't cry anymore dad</u> she said. The other reason I have come is to tell you Jesus is coming soon, "stay ready" were her last words and at that moment the angels put their arms around her arms and they all begin to gently lift upward and away from me.

I stood there gazing upward until I could see them no more. What amazed me was she wasn't that small two-year old baby I held in my arms twelve years ago...she was a young beautiful lady of fourteen years of age. Everything changed about her except for her eyes, hair and smile. When she looked at me her eyes had the twinkle of that two-year old who used to stare at me as I played with her all the while smiling because it brought such joy to me to see her happy.

I lay there on my bed not wanting to lose the moment. I could still smell her fragrance that filled the room and I knew the second I opened my eyes she would be gone, I wanted to capture that treasured moment and never let go. From that point on true healing filled my soul. I often say we can tell when God has healed you because the "sting is gone." Before the vision I could not mention Deanna's name without feeling the sting.

Before the vision I could not hear others speak about my baby because of the sting inflicted in my soul.

Today I can talk of her and yes maybe there is a tear or two but as the Bible says, "Tears bring healing." Some people heal quickly with others it may take time in this case it took me about twelve years to heal and I thank Jesus always for His healing power. David said it best in Psalms 23:3, "He (Jesus) restored my soul..." the soul of man is the reasoning part of man. It is where our emotions flow forth from. It is the mind and heart of all men so in other words David was saying Jesus restored my thinking and He restored my heart.

The old time preachers would say, "Had it not been for the Lord on my side where would I be?" Without the healing virtue of Christ I could have lost my mind. According to the Bible from death, life is given it is nature's way ask any farmer and he'll describe the "seed concept." The seed of life that came from this experience was an album entitled, "Keep Me Strong in the Night." It's a recording of original songs, ten in all that continue to bless people across the land and is requested on a weekly basis even though it is a few years old. Most people complain they can't keep their CD because someone always wants to borrow it and they never return them.

Since then God has blessed me with many more songs that will be recorded. I get excited about God, and how He continues to amaze me. That is the reason I sing, "God you been so good to me." Each time I read this section concerning my daughter tears fill my eyes and for a brief moment I'm overcome with the presence of God. I'm reminded of the countless people who have shared how healing has come into their life because of the testimony… may the blessing of the Lord over shadow your life and you experience healing now in the mighty name of Jesus. Let the tears flow if need be. Amen.

Reading through this book I recognize the hand of God throughout it. It truly is His words that were written, just as He gave the words unto Moses on a stone tablet He has orchestrated all my tests and trials to become a testimony that provides healing for others…myself included.

Conclusion of the Matter

"Pastors, Churches, & Preachers"

Now this is where I get to talk about you. Most times when we hear these names we think someone is going to take up an offering this is not the case here. Through out my travels I have been blessed to meet some very outstanding people and minister in some very special churches. Recently I just learned a saying, "Blessed are the short winded for they will be invited back to preach."

One of the Pastors who played a pivotal role in developing my ministry was Rev. Johnny Iron Shirt. He was different then the other ministers during my early Christian years and he was the answer to my prayers since I was asking God for a 'spiritual mentor' in my life. I actually prayed and asked God to 'give me' a preacher who would teach me how to serve God to the best of my ability and that person was Johnny Iron Shirt.

Our relationship begins with a visit to my home one autumn afternoon and continued until his passing some years back. He would invite me to travel with him and his family on ministry trips in parts of eastern Montana and Washington State, which I considered the highest honor since he was my Pastor and I considered myself to be the least qualified concerning the things of ministry.

The other reason he was different in the manner he conducted himself…you could see the Spirit of God in his life spiritually, physically, and financially. The way he preached from the inside was manifested outside. When others were wearing blue jeans he would show up dressed to the tee in a three-piece suit. Now to a young man on the 'reservation' this made an impression difficult to forget.

During my first ministry trip with him we stopped in Havre, Montana at a restaurant to eat, now for most people this wouldn't be a big deal but in my eyes I thought "this guy is rich" since we just passed a 'greasy spoon' for this elegant restaurant. Romans 12:2a, "And be not conformed to this world; but be ye transformed by the renewing of your mind…" even though I was a Christian my mind was thinking at a poverty level, reservation lifestyle, no hope for tomorrow mindset. I was waiting for the 'round steak' or as it is know bologna (lunch meat) and bread. He told me when you travel always find time to set down and enjoy at least one hot meal…it allows you to relax. Now that I'm the minister and other young men travel with me I practice this principle and it really works.

Some of the stories I heard of the early Native American preaches was breaking down in the 'middle of nowhere' South Dakota or northern Alberta Canada, eating bologna and bread in the car if you were lucky and not knowing where your next dollar was coming from. I guess for some this was their spiritual badge of honor, their war stories in the ministry or either it just made them feel holy. However, this wasn't what I was taught by Pastor John Iron Shirt. He had his own construction business, drove nice cars, and lived in a nice home with a fireplace. He was also a very generous person, which I witnessed on many instances.

As a matter of fact one of those sad Indian ministry stories goes like this; There was this group of people who had just finished preaching on a South Dakota Indian reservation and where preparing to leave for the next engagement. One of the local residents noticed that their tires were totally bald with wire sticking out and mentioned this to the driver, his reply was, "Were not concerned the Lord will take care of us." In those days there were very few paved roads on Indian reservations and as the group raced down the gravel road a tire blew out causing the vehicle to run into the ditch and then to the other side of the road before stopping.

After the dust settled and the screams of panic subsided (Jesus, Jesus, Jesus) and to their dismay all in the car found they were safe. As they begin to check the tires they discover none of them were flat. Confused, mystified, and shaken someone opened the cars trunk…the old beaten, bald spare in the trunk had exploded for whatever reason causing the driver to react as if a tire on the vehicle had blown out and automatically he went for the ditch. I guess you're supposed to do that if a tire blows…or not.

When I was a Youth Pastor I was asked to minister on the Crow Indian reservation for the first time. The meeting was held at an out door stadium used for major rodeos during the "Crow

Fair." As a young minister I was taken in awe that I was given this opportunity because of the ministry line-up. The Pastor who invited me was Myron Falls Down, a former basketball star and college educated minister. From that time to this I have considered him my close friend. We may not see each other regularly however, when we do it is as if we just walked out the door and then returned again to continue our visits or spiritual meals together.

Pastor Myron Falls Down is truly a man of God without compromise who is an established leader among the Crow Nation and throughout Indian Country as well as parts of Canada. Through his example Myron taught me that a person could remain faithful to God while serving the people. On a personal note, Myron is always well dressed…not over dressed when he ministers the Word. He is a minister with passion willing to extend beyond the Crow reservation as he declares, "Jesus is Lord."

Since that time I have ministered at his church in Wyola, Montana where I have witnessed first hand how the Holy Spirit is truly allowed to move during the service. Because of his business proficiency I learned how to treat visiting ministers with genuine hospitality. Myron always provided lodging in a nearby town since Wyola is isolated between Sheridan, Wyoming and Hardin, Montana just off of exit 544 on Interstate 90. Plus he always ministered to our needs when the meeting was concluded. These are things they don't teach in Bible school.

If there is any flaw in the man I'm unaware except that each time we meet and after exchanging our greetings he will ask me,

"Bill, how old do I look?" and my reply is always the same, "You don't look that old. You even look younger than the last time I saw you." Like any true man of God, Pastor Myron and his wife Victoria have claimed to the mountain tops and strolled through the spiritual valleys...they have endured the storms of life only to come through with victory and a greater anointing. Just like Joshua of old Myron is always looking for another mountain to conquer for the kingdom of God.

Reverend Gabriel Yellow Owl is my friend period. Anyone who knows me knows Brother Gabe. When I first met Gabe he was a kid (or as we say just a pup) but we quickly became friends later on I was informed by my mother that I was closely related to Yellow Owl's through my grandmother Annie Mad Plume Wall. Whose people are Spotted Bears and the Yellow Owls.

That brings me to this point concerning Blackfeet culture. When you are introduced to someone it isn't your occupation that identifies you as in some cultures (hello my name is...I'm a doctor, lawyer, teacher, etc.). We are introduced as, "This is Bill Old Chief, his parents are...and if that didn't work then they will say and his grandparents are." Even if they don't know you, when your parents or grandparents are mentioned they will say, "Ah...I know you now."

I had the privilege of performing the wedding ceremony for Gabe and Carol in October 1992. Then on February 15, 1998 I witnessed brother Gabe become an ordained minister as his Pastor of Community Christian Center. I have watched their children transform into young adults. I have seen Brother Gabe become a grandfather and it seems we have know each other for just a short time.

In my ministry travels throughout the United States and Canada it was Gabe who stood at my side. When we first begun he was my drummer and to this day I haven't found one that matches his ability and gifting as a drummer. Somewhere between our travels he matured into an awesome bass and guitar player. Music just seems to jump on him. If called upon to minister he is full of the word and can preach with the best of them.

His love for children has compelled him and Carol into coaching the youth in Great Falls, Montana in the arena of boxing, which they have done for a number of years. This has taken them to the Olympic try outs in Colorado Springs several times producing young warriors with a vision of gold and the honor of representing their country.

Like all true friends it isn't money or material gain that has kept us together, it is the mutual respect we have for each other. We just enjoy being around each other. We laugh together. We cry together. We rejoice together. Just a few years ago one of Gabe's sisters passed away and he asked me to officiate the funeral. During that time I recalled all that we had been through and was thankful that I could be there for his family during their time of loss.

My mind drifted back to a point in my life when trouble seemed to be present and we were coming back from a Promise Keepers event in Seattle, Washington. I was laying in the backseat of the vehicle reading and maybe half asleep when he spoke these words as if speaking to himself out loud, "Next year Bill you will be on that platform ministering." I thought to myself I'm I that bad off that my buddy has to make me fell good by saying that? I didn't say a word as he continued to drive us home.

There are times in our life that God is speaking to us but we just don't have the faith to receive, this was one of those moments. Gabe believed and spoke the word on my behalf I just laughed within like Sarah when told she would conceive a child in her old age. In our minds we try and reason why would God do such a thing or how could God do it?

The following year we had gathered more than sixty men from our reservation to join us a return trip back to Seattle since we were so impressed with what we witnessed the following year… we just wanted everyone to be blessed. Long story short, that Saturday afternoon I was asked to join the other ministers on the Promise Keepers platform and pray a prayer as a Native American representative.

How they choose me out of 65,000 plus men remains a mystery, I just know when God says He is going to do something it will come to pass, whether we believe it or not. I recall sitting across from Bishop Porter of Denver, Colorado as he was instructing the rest of the ministry team. I was thinking, "How did I get here" over and over again I was saying that in my mind and as if I said it out loud Bishop Porter stopped addressing the others, looked directly at me and said, "Pastor Old Chief you are here because

God ordained you to be here." He then continued talking to the others.

I can't talk about Gabe without recalling a time I was "pushing" him away because I wanted to protect him. It was a negative period of my ministry with doors closing and accusations flowing like Niagara Falls. I was stepping out of my traditional religious comfort zone and some people didn't like it. I was fellowshipping with those who were not Pentecostal and church leaders were mad at me. One evening I was riding with Brother Gabe and I told him, "You need to leave and go own your own" and for a brief moment he bought into it until the Holy Ghost rose up in him and he replied, "God put me with you and until God tells me to go I'm staying with you." Well that was the end of that. Even today we travel proclaiming the Gospel of Jesus to the nations.

Whenever Brother Gabe and I unite and once again explore the Gospel Road. Our stories recant the times we traveled south to Tijuana, Mexico then to northern and western Alberta, Canada or eastern Saskatchewan near the Manitoba boarder. Our journeys have taken us throughout the state of Montana to every Indian reservation and many non-Indian churches and as far south as Atlanta, Georgia on "Stone Mountain" and west into Washington, Idaho, and Oregon. And when we do travel I'm reminded of Joshua and Caleb, David and Jonathan, Peter and John as they all proclaimed, "God is with us."

The only thing is when he rides with me now there is the smell of "Bengay" what's up with that?

In Philippians 4:11b Paul said, "For I have learned, in whatsoever state I am, there with to be content." The subject found in Ephesians 4:11-12 is where God calls individuals into specific function of ministry (Spiritual Gifts) such as Apostles, Prophets, Evangelist, Pastors, and Teachers...notice it begins with Apostles (see 1 Co.12:28) who and can function in all of the callings since Apostles serve in reality as the leaders of the Church because of the particular Message Jesus Christ has given to them.

In my Christian walk I have operated in these Gifts one time or another, sometimes they will overlap. I was first called to be a Youth Pastor at the age of twenty-four then an Associate Pastor three years later. Then Pastor of "Blackfeet Gospel Sound Ministries" there after we established "Community Christian Center" and watched it grow under the direction of the Holy Spirit. Most recently we were Pastors of Four Winds Assembly of God. In my heart I knew I wasn't going to Pastor one church for the rest of my life but the "Heart of a Pastor" never leaves me.

In between serving as a Pastor I was ministering across the county in the position of an Evangelist. The anointing to evangelize is different than a Pastor but comes from the same God. God gives you greater insight and the ability to believe (faith, gifts of healing, working of miracles, word of wisdom, word of knowledge, discerning of spirits) because of the greater number of people you come into contact with and the needs they present.

During my times as a Pastor I would often begin to be moved by the Holy Spirit to present special teachings that were a revelation to me. I noticed that a special anointing and the Spirit of Revelation

(Eph.1:17) would come upon me during this time as I operated in the Office of a Teacher. This anointing is different then teaching Sunday school or a Wednesday night Bible study, both could be taught with a teacher's handbook. The anointing for a Teacher brings forth revelation in the spirit of the hearer.

As the Prophet I have seen this gift overlap both as a Pastor and Evangelist. As a Prophet, God speaks through you (prophecy, word of knowledge, word of wisdom) and the words are inspired from God to the receiver, it is supernatural communication of either present or future events. This is totally different that when a person gives a word in tongues and another translates what was said. This happens as the Holy Ghost wills

Recently Pastors have been calling me something different and each time they mention the name I never comment since I feel uncomfortable being called an Apostle. For the past five years I have been encouraging churches, ministries and individuals because of a specific word I believe is from God and without realizing a Pastor not long ago said, "Bill you are an Apostle" then went on to say why. During the New Year I was ministering on the Crow Indian reservation and the Pastor introduced me as, "Pastor, Evangelist, and Apostle Bill Old Chief." Today I received a letter from a respected elder Pastor in Washington State and splashed across his envelope was "Apostle William Old Chief."

I for one have never been into titles but as my dad would say, "Your gift will make room for you." Paul said I have learned to be content in any state, whatever they call me I just want to be in the will of God. The Five –Fold Ministry is for the maturing [equipping] of the Saints, for the work of the Ministry, for the building up of the Body of Christ. My life is the ministry.

This book would not be complete without mentioning by brother, Dr. Patrick "Titus" Calf Looking a Pastor in his own right and probably one of the most intelligent men I have ever known however, he was a down to earth person who loved Jesus with all his heart.

I met Pat at a Promise Keepers meeting and from that moment we became friends, traveling companions, and schoolmates since we graduated on the same day at the University of Montana. Wherever I ministered there you would find Pat supporting me in the "Amen corner." One autumn day in 2006 at the age of 45 the angels ushered him home. I often think about my friend who would likely be waiting for the first copy of this book and with that in mind I dedicate this to Pastor Titus Calf Looking. My brother. My friend.

These ministries and individuals I would like to give
honor to, for they have been a blessing and encouragement
in my ministry and deserve recognition for their love
and faithful commitment in the service of the Lord.

Father Ed Kolher (my friend)
Little Flower Parish
Browning, Montana

Pastor Rowland Freeman (Blackfeet at heart)
Missoula, Montana

Pastor Merle and Rose Williams (spiritual father & mother)
Marysville, Washington

Pastor Roy & Honey Wolf Tail
Church on the Rock
Browning, Montana

Pastor Myron & Victoria Falls Down
Wyola, Montana

Pastor Gordon Monroe
Browning, Montana

Pastor Dean & Annie Buffalo
Spirit of God Church
Ronan, Montana

Rev. Gabe & Carol Yellow
Great Falls, Montana

Pastor George and Mardell
Abundant Life Church
Grangeville, Idaho

Brother Jerry & Linda Burgin
Yakima, Washington

Pastor Art & Karen Reynolds
Naches, Washington

My Mother and Prayer Warrior
Irene Old Chief
Browning, Montana

Patricia "Pat" & Shawn
My sister and brother in law
"Their heart is always open to me"

My brother Gayle
My sister Rosemary
My sister Darlene

To my sons Billy Dean & Shawn and my daughters Karrilyn
& Kimberly Kash and especially Jaina whom I love with
all my heart and puts a smile on my face each day
Jaina's quote, ("I love you dad to the moon and back.")

For additional books or copies of the music CD "Keep Me Strong in the Night" you can contact us at the following:

Pastor Bill Old Chief
P.O. Box 1586
Browning, Montana 59417
blackfeetleader@gmail.com

If you desire change in your life please pray with me now:
"Heaven Father I come before you in Jesus name. I'm tired of living
my life without you and realize I need you as my Savior. You
alone are able to change my horrible situation and bring me peace
because of the Cross of Calvary and forgive me of my sin through
the blood you shed for me. I choose to serve you this day with all
of my heart. I denounce my former lifestyle and give unto you my
life from this moment on. Be Lord of my life and I will witness to
others of your amazing grace. I believe in Jesus name. Amen."

Numbers 6:24-26 (NLT)

May the LORD bless you
and protect you.
May the LORD smile on you
and be gracious to you.
May the LORD show you his favor
and give you his peace.

Printed in the United States
By Bookmasters